TENNESSEE DAY IN ST. LOUIS

Peter Taylor

TENNESSEE DAY IN ST. LOUIS

A COMEDY

RANDOM HOUSE

NEW YORK

FOR

my mother and
father

CAST OF CHARACTERS

JAMES TOLLIVER, *a St. Louis banker*

HELEN, *his wife*

LANNY, *their son*

JIM, *another son*

WILLIAM, *brother of Helen*

LUCY MCDOUGAL, *William's secretary*

MISS BETTY PETTIGRU, *cousin of James*

MRS. FLORENCE BLALOCK, *companion to Miss Betty*

SENATOR CAMERON CASWELL, *cousin of Helen*

NANCY, *granddaughter of Senator Caswell*

BERT, *the Tollivers' houseboy*

The Time: January 8, 1939

The Place: The entire action takes place in James Tolliver's
house in St. Louis.

There are four acts

ACT
ONE

ACT ONE

A large rectangular room in JAMES TOLLIVER'S *house in St. Louis. Above the fireplace at the left end of the room a Seth Thomas mantel clock ticks noisily. It is the only article of furnishing in evidence which does not seem altogether appropriate to a luxurious game and sitting room of the period between the two world wars. In the room* MISS BETTY PETTIGRU *and* MRS. FLORENE BLALOCK *are occupied with a jigsaw puzzle.* MRS. BLALOCK, *known to all as* FLO DEAR, *is seated at a card table on which the puzzle is spread out—the table being placed a little left of center, downstage; and except at times when her attention is drawn away by the conversation, she works almost feverishly at the puzzle before her.* MISS PETTIGRU, *known to the children in the family as* AUNTIE BET, *stands looking over her companion's shoulder and sometimes glancing through the wide doorway which is in the center of the rear wall.*

Beyond that doorway SENATOR CAMERON CASWELL, *a house guest of the* TOLLIVERS, *can be seen at intervals, as he paces back and forth along the hallway there. Twice, before either of the ladies speaks, this old gentleman passes the doorway. As he passes he is speaking rather emphatically and making exaggerated gestures with his large hands. His words, however, are not perhaps entirely audible to the two ladies or to the audience. Each time he strides past,* AUNTIE BET *and* FLO DEAR *turn their faces toward him and then turn back to the puzzle.*

3

SENATOR CASWELL

The most frightful of all spectacles, the strength of civilization without its mercy . . . (*Reappearing*) It was artfully contrived by Augustus, that, in the enjoyment of plenty, the Romans should lose the memory of freedom.

AUNTIE BET

Genius at work . . . He wrote his lecture on the train, and now he's memorizing it. Could this piece go there?

FLO DEAR

No, I think not.

AUNTIE BET

(*Very slowly*)

If you observed, Flo Dear, the sizable meal he ate when he arrived last night, you'll be as shocked as I was to learn he had already consumed one dinner on the train. Try this.

FLO DEAR

No, it won't go . . . He had eaten on the diner?

AUNTIE BET

A five-course dinner! Everything from Vichyssoise to pecan pie. I overheard the granddaughter telling Helen. I strongly suspect that is why the granddaughter was sent along with him —to prevent such intemperance. But how ineffectual she is!

FLO DEAR

She's a mere child . . . No, no, Betty, you can't force them to fit . . . Her name is Nancy.

4

SENATOR CASWELL

(*Passing doorway*)

A simple, artless country fellow stands before you, my friends.
(*Exit.*)

AUNTIE BET

(*Turns away peevishly, sees* SENATOR CASWELL *passing the doorway, turns back*)

Nancy's a mere child, but *he's* a very knowing old nonagenarian.

FLO DEAR

Betty, he isn't that old. He's only eighty-six.

AUNTIE BET

Well, old octogenarian, old . . . old Southerner! Of the very
worst kind! I strongly suspect he brought Nancy along to make
a match with Jim. Yes, I strongly suspect that!

FLO DEAR

In that case, judging from last evening, she is not so ineffectual, Betty. He waited two hours for her to get dressed, and
waited like a lamb. And I never did hear them come in.

AUNTIE BET

Here? Will this fit?

FLO DEAR

(*Cross*)

No, no!

AUNTIE BET

Well, do hurry with the puzzle, Flo Dear. (*Turning and walking to fireplace, left*) I had made a little wager with Helen about it. I bet her we'd have it done when she gets back from market.

FLO DEAR

(*Dropping pieces of puzzle*)
You bet money on my jigsaw puzzle!

AUNTIE BET

Ah, just to humor Helen, Flo Dear. Only a quarter. It relaxes her to have a bet on when there is a crisis.

FLO DEAR

(*Thoughtfully*)
Yes, yesterday I heard her betting with her own houseboy about how many windows he could wash in an afternoon. As you say, "Only a quarter!" But how many quarters have we seen gambled in this house?

AUNTIE BET

It is only their way of making life interesting. And with this hectic week end ahead we must help Helen in whatever way we can.

(SENATOR CASWELL *passes slowly, gesturing and looking straight ahead.*)

SENATOR CASWELL

Every generation has its crisis, my friends! But preparation for defense does not always mean war!

(*Exit.*)

AUNTIE BET

Dreadful man.

FLO DEAR

(*In a whining voice, working at puzzle again*)

Helen won't let us help in household matters. She says she prefers competition from us in games rather than in homemaking. Probably that's right when there's more than one woman in the house.

AUNTIE BET

(*Looking toward doorway*)

If you live out of the South a few years you forget what Southern politicians are like. You forget what Southern *men* are like.

FLO DEAR

As for me, I dislike competitiveness in all things. I like to work alone at my painting and my needlepoint and at an occasional puzzle—when there is no betting involved!

(*She drops piece of puzzle again and rises from the chair.*)

SENATOR CASWELL

.... Our dreams and our aspirations ...

(*Exit.*)

AUNTIE BET

(*With feeling*)

Until last year he had never put foot in this house! For ten years he has been in and out of St. Louis—ever since his retirement from politics—and yet last year was the first time he had

7

ever crossed James' and Helen's threshold. He was in this house for fifteen minutes, and in half that time he discovered he was a so-called blood relation of Helen's.

FLO DEAR

(*Sweetly*)

That was *very* Southern of him, wasn't it?

AUNTIE BET

It was very country and backwoodsy of him! But those adjectives are synonymous with Southern. I learned that early in life, before I had ever seen anything that wasn't Southern.

FLO DEAR

(*Picking at puzzle again, standing*)

Nevertheless, it is a genuine kinship he has discovered, Betty. I have looked it up in the Annals of East Tennessee. He is actually the same kin to Helen that you are to James. He's—

AUNTIE BET

(*Returning to table*)

Genuine or not, it is an old story with the Senator! And it is a standing joke with all the Tennessee people who live here. Every single member of the Tennessee Society knows how he does: if he calls you cousin one year, you can count on him as your house guest the next. He never fails to turn up for the Society's banquet, and this is the third year he has been speaker of the evening. Every year he discovers a new cousin.

SENATOR CASWELL

. . . I plead guilty to the soft impeachment . . .
(*Exit.*)

FLO DEAR

Has it occurred to you that he might hear what we are saying?

AUNTIE BET

A man eighty-four years old has no business hearing that well. He has no business eating so much, either, or striding about the way he does. And this granddaughter he brought with him! (*Sotto voce*) He has been coming to St. Louis for ten years, but this is the first time anyone has ever set eyes on a member of his real family.

FLO DEAR

Nancy seems to be a nice girl. She went to school in Nashville.

AUNTIE BET

We *all* went to school in Nashville! That's no excuse. If Senator Caswell were intimate enough to invite himself here this way he would have known that today is little Lanny's birthday and James' and Helen's anniversary (*With sarcasm*) as well as Tennessee Day. Now everybody is forbidden to mention the birthday or the anniversary for fear of embarrassing the old . . . the old coot! the old covite! the old cohee!
(*She twists a piece of the puzzle violently.*)

FLO DEAR

(*Springing from her chair*)
Ah, Betty, you've broken that piece! And it was the shape of

a Gerrymander! . . . You're beside yourself, Betty. Shame on you. (AUNTIE BET *turns her back, later turns around again*) You couldn't sleep last night for thinking about this. I heard you when you got up and took those shameless pills. Shame on you. And all out of jealousy for the poor old Senator who will be here but a few days. They have taken him in only for a few days, Betty; they've taken us in for life.

(*They stand looking at each other. The only sound is that of the clock's ticking.* SENATOR CASWELL *passes the doorway slowly, and for the first time peers in at the two ladies, who this time do not observe him. Exit* SENATOR CASWELL *with the first sound of* JAMES' *and the others' entering.*

Enter JAMES TOLLIVER *and his son from extreme right. They are followed by* BERT, *the houseboy, carrying an enormous brown-paper package which contains a set of golf clubs.* JAMES *also carries a package.*)

JAMES

Put the clubs in the closet, Bert.

BERT

Yes, sir. I'm certainly sure they must be beautiful. Miss Helen will *love* some new clubs.

JAMES

They are not for Miss Helen. They are for Lanny.

BERT

You don't say?

JAMES

Here, we'll put everything in the closet and lock the door.

AUNTIE BET

(*Crossing to* JAMES, *finger to lips, pointing toward center door-way*)

Sh-sh. Genius at work! Very ancient genius.

JAMES

I know. That's why we came in the side door. Helen and Lanny aren't here, are they?

AUNTIE BET

No, and Helen left word *he* was to have the whole front part of the house to pace about in. It seems he can't memorize his lecture without pacing through all the rooms and hallways in the house. (FLO DEAR *sits down at the table again, and looks blankly at the puzzle.* JIM *crosses from left and sits down opposite her*) He is only supposed to speak for twenty minutes, and yet it has taken him all morning to set his speech to memory.

JIM

(*In an affected "Eastern" voice, hardly moving his lips when he speaks*)

Who says he will speak only twenty minutes, Auntie Bet? Who'll stop him once he gets on his feet?

JAMES

What are you mumbling, Jim?

JIM

I said—

JAMES

Yes, I heard you. But who'll care to stop him? He will have an audience made to order. I understand the title of his speech will be "Tennessee Is a State of Mind."

JIM

Too bad Tennessee isn't that, as far as I'm concerned. The last time I saw Tennessee it looked like a state of wilderness.

FLO DEAR

Ji-im, dear!

AUNTIE BET

(*Laughing*)
Did you hear what Jim said, James?

JAMES

Of course not. No one but you and Flo Dear can understand Jim's muttering . . . Wait, Bert. Jim, let's show Auntie Bet and Flo Dear what we bought for Lanny's birthday.
(BERT *brings out the package.*)

JIM

What *we* bought, Father? What *you* bought. Father can't pass a sporting goods store without buying something. Today just happens to be Lanny's birthday, and so he bought him a set of golf clubs.

AUNTIE BET

But, James, little Lanny doesn't care for golf. Why, he's quite funny on the subject.

JAMES

(*Annoyed*)

Who thinks he's funny on the subject? *You* and Flo Dear ...
Don't open them, Bert. Put them back.

(BERT *returns the package and makes his exit, right.*
JAMES *locks the door to the closet and puts the key in his*
pocket.)

JIM

Auntie Bet, in this family people buy other people only what
they would like to have for themselves. (*Working at puzzle*)
Where is that lovely Nancy?

FLO DEAR

She's at market with your mother and Lanny.

AUNTIE BET

Now, what's become of the Senator? He has been prancing
up and down that hall all morning. From the solarium to the
library and back again. Flo Dear even suggested that he may
have been eavesdropping on us.

FLO DEAR

No, Betty, I only raised the question!

JAMES

(*Who has moved downstage right*)

Auntie Bet. (*Beckoning*) There is something I'd like to confer with you about before Helen comes in.

(AUNTIE BET *joins him.* JIM, *who is seated at the card table*
with FLO DEAR, *facing left, turns his head to try to hear*
his father.)

13

FLO DEAR

It is a very difficult puzzle, isn't it, Jim?

(JIM *turns his attention back to the puzzle, and they both work away. As they do so and as* JAMES *and* AUNTIE BET *confer,* SENATOR CASWELL *enters silently and approaches the card table.* JIM *and* FLO DEAR *watch him without speaking, as though hypnotized, as he first studies the puzzle a moment and then begins methodically, even rhythmically, to fit the remaining pieces of the puzzle together. Meanwhile,* JAMES *and* AUNTIE BET, *downstage, speak in lowered voices.*)

JAMES

Has my esteemed brother-in-law been around the house this morning?

AUNTIE BET

No, William left for his office even before you and Jim got off.

JAMES

I mean, has he been back?

AUNTIE BET

Not that I know of. No, I'm sure he has not. (*Indifferent*) But Miss McDougal has called twice from his office.

JAMES

Yes, she called me at the Bank, too . . . Something's in the wind. My opinion, Auntie Bet, is that Helen's Brother William is about to skip out on us, *and* on Lucy McDougal.

AUNTIE BET

You mean move out? Give up his room here? Never! That would mean spending some of his own money, James. I strongly suspect he won't.

JAMES

From the looks of his account at the Bank it appears he's going to spend all of his money. And he has a great deal, you know.

AUNTIE BET

Well, you certainly don't want to prevent his leaving us, do you, James? What's one brother-in-law more or less in this house? Why, the Senator can move into his room and settle here permanently. *That* would be lovely.

JAMES

If William is leaving us, why of course it's his own business. But I mean to prevent his doing so until after this week end.

AUNTIE BET

You're thinking of Helen?

JAMES

Yes, and I'm thinking of Jim. Somehow or other, Jim is involved. That's why I insisted upon his going to the Bank with me this morning. He was supposed to be back at Princeton on Thursday, and I am convinced his staying over the week end is connected with—with whatever adventure his uncle is up to.

AUNTIE BET

Shame on you, James. Jim stayed over for your anniversary and for Lanny's birthday, though that has all been ruined.

JAMES

And I'm thinking of Lanny. It will have an awful effect on Lanny if William abandons Lucy McDougal ... I'm thinking of us all; and I intend to do what I can to keep Brother William here through Sunday.

AUNTIE BET

Mark my word, you will have your chance. He'll be here for one more free meal ... (*Enter* WILLIAM, *center. He moves slowly toward the group at the card table*) ... What did I tell you? And if his secretary is not with him, it will be our first Saturday lunch without *her*.

JAMES

Oh, Lucy McDougal will be here. I have seen to that.
  (*As his uncle enters,* JIM *rises from the card table and thereafter watches* WILLIAM's *every move.* WILLIAM *and* SENATOR CASWELL *shake hands.*)

WILLIAM

I heard you speak once when I was just a small kid, down in Tennessee, Cousin Cameron. You were making a race for something or other, I reckon. I never thought then you were my cousin, or, at least, that I would ever shake your hand and call you "Cousin."
  (*He turns his back abruptly and speaks to* JIM *in an undertone.*)

JAMES
(Sotto voce)

Such rudeness.

AUNTIE BET

(Raising her voice and speaking from downstage, right)
Senator Caswell, I hope that our female chatter in here did
not disturb you this morning.

SENATOR CASWELL

On the contrary, my dear lady. The sound of feminine voices
always helps me to concentrate.

(JIM *bursts into laughter, the affected quality of his
speech carrying over into his laughter.*)

SENATOR CASWELL

Don't misunderstand me. I feel that all's right with the world
when there is the sound of women's voices in the house. When
my wife was alive and our daughters were still at home—we
had all girls—I asked for nothing better than to have them in
the room with me chatting away while I was in the throes of
composition. And when I had to memorize something for the
lecture platform, I used to stroll from room to room watching
the girls and their mother at their various tasks and entertain-
ments. (*He and* AUNTIE BET *have moved toward each other and
now stand face to face, center*) Later on, after my wife's death,
and before the girls had married, I used to like nothing better
than to have the girls gather in my room after I was in bed and
talk there together until I fell off to sleep. There was no sweeter
moment in life.

FLO DEAR

What a lovely picture, Senator Caswell. My father was very much the same, wasn't he, Betty?

AUNTIE BET

So I have heard you say, Flo Dear. My own father was certainly not like that. His only thought concerning me was to find me a rich husband. There was nobody rich enough in Nashville, and so he used to take me, in the summertime, to every resort from the mountains of Virginia to the State of Maine in search of marriageable money. In the end, he couldn't even find me a poor man . . . But since the Senator is so fond of femininity, Flo Dear, I think it behooves us to freshen up before lunch.

FLO DEAR

Yes, the puzzle is finished.

AUNTIE BET

Good girl, Flo!

FLO DEAR

(*As they go out*)
It wasn't I. It was the Senator.

WILLIAM

Jim, I want you to come up to my room with me for a minute.
(*Exeunt* JIM *and* WILLIAM. JAMES' *eyes follow them out the door, center. He even starts to speak, but then he only stands staring through the doorway a moment after they have gone.* SENATOR CASWELL *strolls to left end of room*

and stops near the fireplace. From there he gazes at
JAMES, *who presently turns around and walks slowly*
toward him.)

SENATOR CASWELL

(*Gesturing toward center doorway*)
Those are your two older boys, James?

JAMES

Heavens, no, Senator! Jim's my boy. That's Helen's brother
ou just met, but he is a member of our household here. *He's*
ess than ten years younger than I am.

SENATOR CASWELL

Ah, yes. It is sometimes hard to keep one's relatives straight,
sn't it?

JAMES

(*Opening large panel in rear wall, left, showing built-in re-*
frigerator and bar equipment)
Indeed, it is. Would you like a little toddy before lunch,
Senator?

SENATOR CASWELL

Ah, about three fingers of whiskey on some ice. That's a
marvelous modern arrangement you have there, James ... And
people wonder why I am so fond of coming here to this mag-
nificent city of yours. Why, you have everything here.

JAMES

Well, we have all that is modern and citified, but—

SENATOR CASWELL

Ah, you have more than that! In the midst of the delights which the modern city offers, you have the delights of the old-fashioned country family. You have your Negro servants and your children and your dependent kinfolks all about you here in one house.

JAMES

(*Laughing*)

Is that how it appears to you, Cousin Cameron?

SENATOR CASWELL

But isn't it really so, now, James?

JAMES

Well, it would *seem* so, I must admit . . . Is that about right?

SENATOR CASWELL

Ah, exactly. Exactly. (*Taking a sip*) And even this! Why, it must be Jack Daniel's.

JAMES

None other. I brought it up from the cellar for your special delectation. I have quite a cellar, sir, and would enjoy showing it to you while you are here.

SENATOR CASWELL

Delighted . . . You see, James, I feel that all my friends here make up a sort of microcosm of life back home.

JAMES

And do you prefer the microcosm to the real thing?

SENATOR CASWELL

In a sense, yes. Perhaps it's the verisimilitude itself I relish. Yes, the verisimilitude. It is as though I can really have my cake and eat it too. I can enjoy all the familiar patterns, all the cherished paraphernalia of my long life yet without the ... responsibility. I have all these friends and relatives here, and yet I never get to know the friends *too* well, and the relatives are never *too close kin* for comfort.

JAMES

I begin to understand you.

SENATOR CASWELL

(*Turning up his glass*)

Yes, here there seem to be all of the pleasant aspects of our way of life, and none of the—the less pleasant aspects. This may be only an illusion, but it seems to me that most of what was bad has gone out of family life in the new America. People now seem free to take only whatever was good about it and to discard the rest. The young people seem to be loved by their families, yet it is not that kind of love which was heaped upon you till you felt that you could not move a limb without shifting the whole world. It is not primarily as a Southerner that I am speaking, but as an old-fashioned person. It is the same everywhere in America. The old-style American had, of necessity, to be first a Southerner or a New Englander or a Midwesterner. That went without saying.

JAMES

Yes, that's so ... May I fix you another?

SENATOR CASWELL

Ah, yes, since today is Andy Jackson Day! A quick one in memory of the Grandee of Tennessee! ... Helen and my granddaughter will be coming in directly?

JAMES

Any moment.

SENATOR CASWELL

A quick one, then ... Yes, it is the verisimilitude. The verisimilitude makes a strong appeal to the poet in me. I began life as something like a poet, James ... Thank you, thank you. (*Sips drink*) Most men in public life began as lawyers. I began as a kind of actor and literary man. I gained my livelihood by lecturing. I traveled the length and breadth of the land on the lecture platform before I was thirty years old. (*Turns up glass*) When I retired from public life a dozen years ago, it was my intention to pick up my youthful career where I had left off ... But I found that there was no longer a demand for that kind of thing. You know, the radio and the moving pictures, they have altered everything. There is no longer an audience for my kind of performance.

JAMES

You'll find a most appreciative audience tonight, I'm sure.

SENATOR CASWELL

Ah, sometimes the Southerners one meets out of the South seem more Southern than the South.

JAMES

(Laughing quietly)

Yes, I'm afraid so.

SENATOR CASWELL

A wonderful thing.
     (He hands his glass to JAMES.*)*

JAMES

(Politely)

Another?

SENATOR CASWELL

Two fingers. (JAMES *turns to the bar*) I often compare the people I know in this fine city to the elegant little colony of Virginians who found themselves in Paris during the Civil War and became the favorites of the French Court.

JAMES

Well, it's a far cry from that, Senator. We all came here to make money, you know, and came of our own free will. It is mostly shoes, insurance and banking with us.

SENATOR CASWELL

(Accepting glass)

But it is the quality of the home life I am speaking of principally. I hope you won't mind if I mention the atmosphere of this house in my lecture tonight.

JAMES

(Smiling)

Before you do that, sir, I think I should set you straight on a couple of points. Neither my cousin, whom we all call Auntie Bet, nor her companion, Mrs. Blalock, is in any sense a dependent of ours. They used to visit us here in the good days of the twenties, and when the bad days of the thirties came, Auntie Bet, who is a woman of considerable property, insisted upon their moving up here from Nashville. They didn't come as paying guests, but during the worst days of the depression Auntie Bet paid the salaries of servants we would otherwise have let go, she kept up the house in the style to which it was accustomed, she provided all manner of luxury for us. I should never have permitted it, but, Senator, I have grown fond of all the things I hardly knew existed when I was a boy in the country. And I am afraid I have let my two boys be spoiled beyond endurance. (JAMES *pauses.* SENATOR CASWELL, *who has been sipping his drink, suddenly empties it. His attention has already seemed to wander. Now he sits down, rests his head on the back of the couch, and closes his eyes*) As for my wife's brother, he is certainly independent of us now. As far as hard cash goes, he could buy and sell us all. He was one of the irresponsible young men of the twenties—in his own country way. He is a reckless sort of fellow, a kind of lone wolf, whom none of us understands and some of us dislike. In a way he is like something left over from the old frontier in Andy Jackson's time. When I was beginning as a small town banker in the twenties, at a time when there was money everywhere, Brother William was little more than a bum. He wouldn't finish his schooling. It may be he couldn't. Other boys used to call him a blockhead. He threw away the money and the property his father had left him. Half the time his own sister didn't know where he could be found. If he worked at all it was likely to be as a day laborer somewhere. There was a period—more than one period, in fact—when he became a real liquor head. Only Lucy McDougal was able to bring him out of that. But finally when times began to get bad all over the country, he was suddenly inspired to try to make money. It was as though he had never thought of it before—that's the kind of fellow he is. He wrote to Helen and me and asked us for shelter, as he put it. I don't believe that until then he had ever asked a relative for anything. He never seemed to have any book sense, but he always had a lot of pride. Anyway, he came here and took a job, on commission, as an insurance and real estate salesman. He managed to use every social connection that we had as well as the acquaintance with the host of people from back home who live here. His country accent and his rough manner seemed to act in his favor and reassure his clients. And, by God, when half the people I know were choosing between bankruptcy and suicide, he began selling life insurance and cheap real estate as nobody else in this town had ever done. And now, by God—

> (*Suddenly he catches himself. He looks at* SENATOR CAS-WELL *for the first time since saying,* "*As far as hard cash goes,*" *and finds him asleep. As he gazes at the old man, he hears the voices of* HELEN, LANNY, NANCY *and* LUCY, *and he turns around to greet them.*
>
> *From right enter* HELEN *and* NANCY, *followed by* LANNY *and* LUCY.)

JAMES

Sh-sh! Genius resting!

25

NANCY

Granddaddy!
(*She bursts into hushed laughter.*)

JAMES

(*Guiltily*)
He dropped off to sleep while I was talking.

HELEN

(*Giving* JAMES *a wifely kiss*)
How could anyone be bored by my captivating husband.
Unless—James, you weren't talking golf to him, or banking?

JAMES

No.

NANCY

You must have been saying something he didn't want to
hear. He always dozes when we try to tell him something he
doesn't want to know.

SENATOR CASWELL

Who says I'm dozing? (*Coming quickly to his feet*) Why,
Helen, we've been awaiting your return. You must have bought
out the whole market. You must, indeed.

NANCY

(*Sotto voce*)
Cousin Helen, that means he would like to know what we
are having for lunch ... (*Seeing his glass*) Why, Granddaddy,

you've had a drink! (*Reproachfully*) Oh, Granddaddy! (*Going to him*) You know you're not supposed to. Not before lunch! And you didn't save me a drop.

HELEN

Oh, oh! It can't be. They finished the puzzle, and I have lost another twenty-five cents to Auntie Bet. Come look at it, Lanny. That piece you said was a cotton field was part of somebody's wig. So you owe *me* a twenty-five cent piece. You can just pay Auntie Bet.

LANNY

(*He has been showing* LUCY *a book*)
Mother, nobody has introduced Lucy to Cousin Cameron.
(*Even while examining the book with* LUCY, *he has been glancing at* SENATOR CASWELL.)

HELEN

Oh, forgive me, Lucy.

LANNY

Cousin Cameron, may I present Miss McDougal. She is my uncle's fiancée, and you'll find her the most interesting member of this family.

(LUCY *comes forward and shakes hands with* SENATOR CASWELL.)

NANCY

(*Giggling*)
Lanny, how priceless you are.

27

LANNY

But it's true. Everyone acknowledges it. She and Flo Dear are the only grown people I know who have read a book in ten years . . . Flo Dear knows an immense amount about genealogy and is always reading something on the subject. She's a professional emblazoner too. She's immensely talented, but nobody appreciates her. She doesn't even appreciate herself.

JAMES

Don't use your hands so much when you talk, Lanny.

HELEN

I thought it was about *Lucy's* accomplishments you were going to tell Nancy. He's forgotten you, Lucy.

LUCY

I'm not in a class with Flo Dear, I assure you.

LANNY

(*To* NANCY)

Oh, Lucy reads everything. And appreciates everything.

LUCY

Myself most of all.

LANNY

I've tried her on the most difficult modern poetry, and she breezes through it with no trouble.

(NANCY *explodes with laughter, and* LANNY *turns away from her and walks toward left.* NANCY *follows him a few steps.*)

NANCY

Don't be mad, Lanny. I only laugh at your funny *way* of saying things. You're already my favorite cousin.

LANNY

Yes, likely. What about Jim? I know what time you all came in last night. And how long you stayed downstairs, too.

HELEN

Lanny!

LANNY

(*Suddenly delighted, addressing the whole group*)
They were downstairs for four chapters of *The Decline and Fall of the Roman Empire,* which makes it about three centuries. And that's about right!
(*He is convulsed with laughter.*)

JAMES

Don't laugh at your own jokes, Lanny.

NANCY

He *is* a scream, Cousin James. Up there reading on Saturday night. What *was* it he was reading?

JAMES

Don't spoil him, Nancy. He has been spoiled enough by the women in the family.

HELEN

Ha! It is his father who has spoiled him, Nancy. Lanny, do come look at the puzzle and admit you were wrong about the cotton field. (LANNY *moves back toward card table*. NANCY *puts her arm about his shoulder*) You had better have a look. I think maybe it's Napoleon and Josephine.

JAMES

(*With pride*)

Lanny is quite an authority on Napoleon.

LANNY

(*To* HELEN)

Oh, you were faking. You knew it wasn't Bonaparte. It's Washington's farewell to his mother.

HELEN

So that's who that old lady is. I must admit that Lanny knows more than I do about historical pictures.

LANNY

Historical, Mother? (*Laughs superciliously*) That picture should be classed as one of the great mythological paintings.

HELEN

(*With heavy irony*)

Forgive me. Of course you're right, and there is a fine lesson in this myth for you. The General is on his knees before his mother, a picture of humility.

SENATOR CASWELL

(*Who has been watching* LANNY)

With your permission, Helen, I shall, as the ladies say, go to my room and freshen up before lunch.

HELEN

By all means, Cousin Cameron. Lanny, you go along with Cousin Cameron and see that he has everything he needs.

SENATOR CASWELL

(*Obviously repelled by the idea*)

Oh, no. Indeed, no. Indeed, no. I am in need of nothing. I am only going to stretch out across my bed and lose myself for a moment or two, if there is time before lunch.

HELEN

There's time aplenty. I'm afraid we eat a very late lunch on Saturday, Cousin Cameron.

JAMES

I'll go along with the Senator. I'm going up anyway.

HELEN

And Nancy and I must arrange those flowers she bought for the table. They're lovely flowers, but I know no more about flower arrangement than I do about historical pictures.

JAMES

(*Stopping in doorway, center*)

I'll tell William you are down here, Lucy. He and Jim went upstairs just before you came in.

(LUCY *smiles formally. They all go out except* LANNY *and* LUCY. *Neither speaks for a moment. Then—*)

LANNY

(*Furious*)

He'll have no part of me! I guess you noticed that, Lucy.

31

LUCY

(*Mystified*)

Who won't?

LANNY

Cousin Cameron. For some inscrutable reason, I'm poison to him. You saw him refuse to let me go upstairs with him.

LUCY

He didn't want *any*one to go with him, Lanny. He's old and he's proud. He was afraid they would think he couldn't make it alone. Especially since he had had a drink or so.

LANNY

No, he was the same way to me last night when I tried to ask him some questions about the old days back in Tennessee. He ignored me consistently—me, of all people. He doesn't know it was *I* who put the Confederate flag over the mantel in his room. Why, I am the only one here who has any genuine interest in the South and what he might have to say about it.

LUCY

(*Idly*)

Maybe that's because you are the only one of us who has never lived there.

LANNY

I have been counting the days till he would get here. It is really terribly exciting having him here, Lucy. It is like having someone out of the distant past step into the present.

LUCY

(*Her thoughts are wandering, but she laughs*)
The Senator might not appreciate that.

LANNY

Think of all he has lived through, and of the people he has known, or seen, or just been alive with. They say he is eighty-six years old—

LUCY

Who says so?

LANNY

Auntie Bet.

LUCY

She probably exaggerates his age. He can't be that old and as vigorous as he is, Lanny.

LANNY

Well, he's more than eighty, anyway. He must have been almost my age at the end of the Civil War. Think of that! Two of his older brothers were killed at Shiloh.

LUCY

How did you find that out?

LANNY

Oh, one of the questions I asked him last night was, were any of his close relatives killed in the War.

LUCY

That was a pleasant way to begin.

LANNY

Think of all the eventful times he has lived through! And doesn't it excite you to think that when he was born, John C. Calhoun and Henry Clay were still alive? Yet here he is in our house today. He *could* actually have seen Lincoln and Jeff Davis, you know. Or General Forrest and Grant; they both fought in Tennessee.

LUCY

Lanny, there is something *awful* about a boy your age being so preoccupied with your family and things like the Civil War.

LANNY

Oh, that business about *who* was alive *when* is just a kind of game I play. It doesn't always relate to "things like the Civil War." Sometimes I use great artists and writers. For instance, I'll take a date like 1890 and I'll discover that that year Thomas Hardy and Tolstoi and Rudyard Kipling were all alive. When you think of it, it makes you sick to have been born so late.

LUCY

(Laughing)

Lanny, Lanny. I only wish I could have been born a little later than I was.

LANNY

How could anybody wish that? . . . Oh, damn him, what right has he to snub me, just because I am . . . fourteen.

LUCY

You're *fif*teen today, Lanny. Have you forgotten? And I have a present for you.

LANNY

Sh! I said "fourteen" on purpose. We're not mentioning my birthday or the anniversary. It might make Cousin Cameron uncomfortable about being here.

LUCY

Lanny, come here and sit down. You *are* worked up over this visit of the Senator's . . . Your imagination—your terrible imagination, Lanny, is going to be your ruin, somehow.

LANNY

(*Sitting beside her*)

I have stayed awake nights thinking about his coming here. You are going to laugh at me, but I have thought just seeing him would be the answer to a million questions I have had about who I am and about our whole family.

LUCY

(*Horrified*)

About *who* you are, Lanny? And your family? My dear boy, that's no way for a person to think of himself—in terms of his family and where his family came from and what they were there. You are too intelligent a person, Lanny, to think in those terms. I am afraid this is what growing up here, in the house with your Auntie Bet and Flo Dear, has meant for you. And being spoiled so by your own mother and father.

LANNY

(*Rising*)

I know who has given you those ideas. If you are going to accept Uncle William's picture—

LUCY

I am speaking of what I have observed myself, Lanny. But let's not get off the subject. You ought to think of yourself as an individual. You ought to observe the things around you for yourself. That's the only way you will ever discover who you are, in any important sense. Don't worry about what the past was like.

LANNY

You make it sound as though everybody was born in a vacuum.

LUCY

(*Thoughtfully*)

Yes, perhaps I do.

LANNY

(*Turning suddenly to her*)

That's what I like about you, Lucy! You sometimes admit that perhaps *I* am right about something, or could be.

LUCY

(*Giggling*)

Why, everybody in this house always thinks you are right about everything—everybody except your brother and your uncle.

LANNY

No, they don't. Everybody either denies or laughs at any idea I ever have. Yet they never have any ideas themselves. Instead, they have stories and anecdotes.

36

LUCY

But you *love* their stories and their reminiscences about old days in Tennessee. Isn't that what you are referring to?

LANNY

I do like their stories, and I think they mean something. Their stories mean something ... But I don't know what it is.

LUCY

And your Cousin Cameron, you think he has the answer to the riddle of what those stories mean?

LANNY

I think he *is* the answer, if I could just get close enough to see ... He's here in this house, and I will find some way of making him talk to me. Why, when I first heard he was coming, Lucy, I couldn't sleep the first night, and the second night I had a dream in which he came to me and said there is no new South; there is only the old South resurrected with the print of the nails in her hands.

LUCY

(*Laughing*)

Oh, Lanny! You read that somewhere.

LANNY

Wait. That's what I dreamed. And the next day I went to the downtown library and got copies of some speeches he made a long time ago at the Tennessee Centennial, and he said things just like that.

LUCY

(*Rising*)

Don't talk that way, Lanny. Whatever you are, don't be a mystic. I want always to be your friend, Lanny, but I can't stand that kind of talk.

LANNY

(*Throwing himself into a chair, head back, eyes closed*)

The difference between us, Lucy, is that you are what Father calls "one of those modern liberals," and I am a traditionalist. *I* am a reactionary!

LUCY

I don't think you know what those words mean yet, Lanny. But let me give you this warning: it's a dangerous sign when someone your age calls himself a conservative. Because at twenty-five he is certain to call himself a radical. And at thirty-five—

LANNY

How did you stand when you were my age?

LUCY

I didn't have a thought in my head when I was your age. Not many people do, thank goodness.

LANNY

Well, how did you stand when you had your first thought?

LUCY

I wanted to kick over everything. I was nearly twenty.

38

LANNY

And have you reversed *your* opinions?

LUCY

I guess I have to some extent . . . Your Uncle Brother thinks I have.

LANNY

(*Irritated*)

I wish you wouldn't speak of him as "Uncle Brother" to me. Jim and I never call him that any more. That's kid stuff.

LUCY

(*Changing tone*)

Lanny, you don't remember when I first came to St. Louis, do you?

LANNY

You came when I was four. I remember you at my fifth birthday party. You took me on your lap and got me to eat the snow cream Uncle Brother had fixed. I thought it was too cold.

LUCY

When I *first* came I stayed here in the house for several weeks, till I found an apartment.

LANNY

I remember something about that too. I came into your room one morning and you let me help you comb your hair, and then you combed mine.

39

LUCY

(*Laughing*)

Yes, yours was longer than mine at the time. I had a wind-blown bob, and you still had long curls. Probably you didn't know it, but it was I who finally persuaded your father to cut your curls.

LANNY

At Uncle—Uncle William's instigation, no doubt.

LUCY

Yes, it infuriated him the way your parents and your aunts babied you. He said it was because of the little girl who died. He said your mother and father were ruining your life because of the little girl they lost.

LANNY

And you believed him?

LUCY

I believed him at the time. In those days he and I believed that families were the cause of all mischief in the world. His family had ruined his life by trying to discipline him too much, so we said. And mine had ruined my life just by being so damned poor.

LANNY

And the reason you have always been kind to me is that you felt sorry for me and wanted to save me!

LUCY

Ah, Lanny, you know that's not so. (*Lightly*) You don't remember it, but for you and me it was love at first sight . . .

40

Your father and mother and your aunts may have spoiled you more than I have, Lanny, but they don't love you one bit more. And today I want to tell you some things about myself, because—because this is the time for it.

LANNY

What do you mean? ... You are saying rather absurd things today, Lucy.

LUCY

What I mean is that I want to be sure that you have a clear picture of what I am really like, just in case—

LANNY

(*Alarmed*)

Just in case what?

LUCY

Oh, Lanny, just in case there is an earthquake or some other act of God ... But stop interrupting me; what I am trying to say isn't easy ... I came here almost ten years ago as your Uncle William's secretary. Back home he and I had been sweethearts when we were younger than you are now, Lanny, and by the time we left high school, people were already calling us "engaged." After our school days we drifted along seeing each other all the time for a while, then "breaking up," as we said, then making it up again. Oh, for seven or eight years that went on. I supported my poor family with a secretarial job in the courthouse. And William—William didn't know what he wanted to do with himself. He was obviously a person of temperament, and probably he should have been some kind of artist.

LANNY

(Suddenly jumping from his chair)

Oh, Lucy! Don't be ridiculous! Uncle Brother couldn't even get through high school!

LUCY

Let me finish. William's parents had been hard on him when he was growing up. Parents used to think they *had* to be hard on boys like William. And they had great plans for his education. I think they wanted him to go into politics, the way Southern men who had temperament used to do . . . Then both of them, his mother and father, died within six months of each other the year he was to graduate from high school, and he wouldn't even finish out the year and get his diploma.

LANNY

I know all about Uncle Brother.

LUCY

(Patiently)

But you don't know all about me.

LANNY

Yes, I do, Lucy.

LUCY

I'm afraid you don't. Listen to me. Finally he came up here, and after a few months he wrote me that he was able to afford a secretary.

LANNY

Yes, a secretary, but not a wife!

LUCY

Oh, I couldn't afford to get married then either. I still had my family to support. I knew perfectly well what I was doing. I was no "young girl" even ten years ago.

LANNY

So you came as his secretary and his *fiancée*.

LUCY

Lanny, you manage to make it sound so smutty.

LANNY

Smutty? Why? Why do you say that?

LUCY

Why do I say that? ... This is what I was afraid of! ... You have no right to be so damnably innocent at your age. Your family's kindness to me has been a great unkindness to you ... Don't you see? They have treated me as one of them. With strangers they have continued to introduce me as William's fiancée, while all the time they have known better. Don't you understand *now*? Hasn't it ever occurred to you that my apartment is William's apartment too most of the time ... that we have lived together there?

LANNY

No ... No, it ... it hasn't ever. But, Lucy, I don't care. And you *are* his ... fiancée.

43

LUCY

No, I am not. I never have been, not since we came here.

LANNY

You never planned to get married, not in the beginning even?

LUCY

Not ever. William wanted to live differently from other people. He *was* different from other people, always.

LANNY

You are different too, Lucy.

LUCY

He and I, when we were young—Well, we weren't intellectual about things. We weren't "enlightened." In fact, we were very ignorant. That's part of being American, though—or it was, if it isn't still. Intellectual ideas just don't get through to us unless we happen to grow up among artists of some kind or have some other special influence. Maybe it isn't true in other countries. I hope not . . . But we thought we were depraved and wicked, and that the world around us was right to be the way it was. And if you are convinced that your strongest feelings are wrong when you are young, it makes a difference—all your life . . . We had no "advanced ideas," and yet ours wasn't just the ordinary kind of affair, either. It was right after the Great War, and—

LANNY

Lucy I don't care about this. What's making you tell me? Is he making life hell for you some way now? I know he does sometimes. I can tell . . . He is a brutal person, isn't he? Isn't he, Lucy?

LUCY

(*Sternly*)

I will not talk to you about William. You become completely irrational.

LANNY

Lucy, I love you.

LUCY

Of course you do.

LANNY

No, I mean something worse than that.

LUCY

Lanny, you're play-acting. You're being a child. My boy, I have been a mother to you, in my way.

LANNY

(*Turning away*)

How I hate him. How I hate him. I could kill him gladly for all the times he has made you suffer. I've seen you crying out in the car sometimes on Saturday before the two of you got out and came in. And then today when you came by yourself in a taxi and we met you in the driveway, I knew he had done something bad. Lucy, I won't say anything else that's repulsive to you, but, dear Lucy, if I can help you let me, let me.

(LUCY *weeps*. WILLIAM *enters through center doorway*.)

45

WILLIAM

What's all this about? James said you craved my company, Lucy. (*Her face is hidden in her hands*) Clear out, Lanny. Clear out, I said.

LUCY

(*With a violent gesture*)

Yes, clear out, Lanny!

LANNY

(*Genuinely confused*)

Where shall I go?

(*He turns and stumbles awkwardly, almost falling, then runs from room.* LUCY *watches him. She is serious.* WILLIAM *laughs at first, then, observing* LUCY, *grows serious. For a moment there is only the ticking of the clock, but it should not be as loud as earlier. Whenever there is conversation in the room the noise of the clock should be reduced until it is barely audible.*)

WILLIAM

I wasn't looking for you to be here today, Lucy. What in God's name fetched you?

(*Pause.*)

LUCY

You're going away, aren't you, William? Isn't it natural that I should come to tell you good-bye?

WILLIAM

I don't know what seems natural to you nowadays.

LUCY

I suppose not.

WILLIAM

Anyhow, you had a feeling that I was "going away." That's why you came?

LUCY

Isn't it so, William?

WILLIAM

Hell, yes, I'm clearing out, Lucy. I've made like the St. Louis businessman long enough . . . But where in hell do you think I'm going, Lucy? You wouldn't guess, ever.

LUCY

Where you are going doesn't concern me, does it?

WILLIAM

I've bought only one ticket, if that's what you mean.

LUCY

Doesn't that sound just a little crude and cruel even to your ears?

WILLIAM

Ten years ago you would have "appreciated my directness."

LUCY

Whatever I did come here for today, it wasn't to have one last quarrel with you, William . . . I still have some understanding of what you are like.

(*The ticking of the clock*.)

WILLIAM

Where I am going doesn't make any difference . . . What makes a difference is that at forty I have found something new under the sun.

(*The ticking of the clock.*)

LUCY

Is she pretty?

WILLIAM

So that's what fetched you. You came to get an answer to that. Who do you think it would be?

LUCY

Any of three or four I know about.

WILLIAM

Well, if I took one of *them,* it would be . . . *in*cidental. That's not the kind of venture I have in mind. Lucy, I'm going out to the West Coast and make a pile of money. A lot of money is going to change hands very soon, everywhere. Things are going to start popping, and I've gotten on to the surest thing there is when things start popping. I aim to git dar fustis with the mostis money, but I've got to move fast.

LUCY

And making money is a new thing under the sun?

WILLIAM

The kind of money I'm talking about is—for me. What a damned nut I've been for ten years. Messing around in St.

Louis—just to show people that *I* could make money even in a depression if I put my mind to it. Why, I haven't known what money is. Everybody here has old-timey notions of what being rich is, Lucy.

LUCY

William, I am glad.

WILLIAM

(*Mixing two drinks at the bar*)

That-a-girl.

LUCY

I'm glad if making money has become something to you besides a way of expressing your contempt for everybody who wants to make money and can't.

WILLIAM

You mean for all my kith and kin.

(*The ticking of the clock.*)

LUCY

When you were thirty, William ...

WILLIAM

Chuck it, Lucy!

LUCY

... you came here to *use* some of your family. They had *used* you so terribly, in their own way. I am glad this is over for you. Even if you are going somewhere to make money in some ter-

rible way, I'm glad . . . Maybe it is just because I've been worn
out with waiting to know when this day would come for us.
Little by little, we have—

WILLIAM

God damn it, let's not speechify.

LUCY

No, I didn't come today for that.

WILLIAM

Why in hell *did* you come?

LUCY

I came to say good-bye . . . Not just to you, but to all your
family. I won't be seeing them after you go. And, William, I
shall miss them as much as I'll miss you.

WILLIAM

God, how you have changed.

LUCY

(*Looking down at herself*)
Yes, haven't I? And *you* look just as you did ten years ago.
And you're starting your life over somewhere.

WILLIAM

I wasn't speaking of looks. You know that damn well. Here
you stand talking about my "family" and about "good-bye's."
And about "after I go." . . . After I go! After I go! You try to
make something out of it, it's not. You make it sound like there

was really some place I could go that would get me away from what I hate in—

LUCY

In me.

WILLIAM

Have it your way. *You* have "matured," and I haven't. I still get sick of people and places and things. I still get cold chills up and down my spine when it looks like people and places and things have got a drag on me.

LUCY

Yes, we used to say, "You're yours and I'm mine," didn't we?

WILLIAM

But at some point you stopped being yours. It was coming here to this house every week, year after year, I think.

LUCY

Oh, say it was my aging, William.

WILLIAM

God. Stop harping on that . . . Stop pretending age had anything to do with it . . . You know, and I know, it was coming here and seeing James and Helen with their boys that changed you. You began to think maybe farms were not the only place families still made sense. Families were not such awful, out-of-date things, after all. You never said those things, but I could tell when you began to think them.

LUCY

Perhaps you could tell from the way my cheeks and my breasts were beginning to sag.

(*The ticking of the clock.*)

WILLIAM

It was as if all you had once set yourself against, Lucy, down there in the clay hills of West Tennessee had come and taken hold of you. You went on talking the same way about the things that families did to people. You read books to back the things you said up; but the more bookish you got about it, the clearer it was that you were whistling in the dark.

LUCY

I was trying to hold my man, wasn't I? Hoping he would marry me yet, wasn't I? ... You are not going to spare me anything, are you?

WILLIAM

And then you began to outfit that apartment with antiques. (*He laughs bitterly*) I couldn't believe it at first. And the little week-end place on the River. *That* place! Christ, Lucy, I dreamed one night you and I had a still out there and the revenuers were after us.

LUCY

You should have cut my salary at the office. Then I couldn't have become so bourgeois ... Well, that's all history, William. And so you say to hell with me. We used to promise each other that's what we'd say if one of us got difficult about our relationship. Aren't you going to say it? "To hell with you, Lucy Mc-Dougal. I'm moving on. I don't know just where I'm going, but I've used my connections here to make money when none of *them* could and now I'm moving on to make money off the rest of the world in its misery."

(*The ticking of the clock.*)

WILLIAM

(*Nodding and speaking mechanically*)

To hell with you, Lucy McDougal, I'm moving on, I don't know just where I'm going, and so on and so forth. However you want it.

LUCY

There is only one thing I want now, William. That is for you to stay through this week end.

WILLIAM

Lucy, Lucy. What nonsense you've come to.

LUCY

Just don't ruin today and tomorrow for everybody in this house. This is their day of days, William.

WILLIAM

What drivel, what slush you've learned to talk.

LUCY

It was only to ask you this last favor that I came today.

WILLIAM

I can hardly believe my ears.
    (*The ticking of the clock.*)

Curtain

ACT
TWO

ACT TWO

The game room. It is two-thirty on Saturday afternoon. Voices can be heard from the dining room. Enter NANCY, *followed by* JIM, *from left.*

JIM

They'll be sitting around that table talking for another hour.

NANCY

That's the first time I have ever had wine with a meal . . . What was it, Jim?

JIM

It was the Hungarian equivalent of sauterne. I forget the name. Father says, "Hungarian wines are better than French." He likes to think he has the best of everything, likes to feel that we are living in the lap.

(SENATOR CASWELL'S *voice is momentarily heard above the others' in the dining room.*)

NANCY

Did you ever see anyone eat so much as my grandfather? It's disgusting.

JIM

Did you ever hear anyone talk as much as my family? Their chatter is too revolting to be disgusting.

NANCY

Your uncle doesn't say much.

JIM

He's all right . . . (*Putting his arm around her waist*) And you're all right.

NANCY

(*Moving away*)

Sa-a-ay, Jimmy.

JIM

What's the matter? I'm awfully keen about you, Nancy. I was sincere last night. Weren't you?

NANCY

Heavens, Jim, they'll all be trooping in here in a minute.

JIM

Were you only kidding around last night. I want to know . . . I meant what I said.

NANCY

You didn't say much.

JIM

I never do. I'm like Uncle William in that.

NANCY

You're sweet, Jimmy. But I don't think you are serious about me. You're just a college boy.

JIM

I'm considerably older than you.

NANCY

That's not the point.

JIM

Here's how serious I am.
(*He kisses her, holding the kiss as long as she will let him.*)

NANCY

You think that's serious?

JIM

Then you *were* kidding around. You're another of those Southern gals. That's what I wanted to know.

NANCY

Don't say "Southern gal" to me again. I heard enough of that at the dance last night.

JIM

(*Quickly*)
Oh, they meant that as a compliment. Southern girls go over big in St. Louis.

NANCY

So what? Who wants to go over as a Southern girl? And since when was going over in St. Louis the last word in anything? You all seem to think St. Louis is *really* something.

59

JIM

Oh, it's a dump. The East's a lot better, if that's what you mean.

NANCY

What I mean is—It's easy to see why all Granddaddy's friends here wanted to get away from Tennessee—and Kentucky and Mississippi too, but I can't see how they're content to get only to St. Louis. There's no real difference between this and home.

JIM

Why, it's the money, chile.

NANCY

That's all *you* know about it, my fine Princeton friend.

JIM

(*Putting his arms around her*)

Meaning you know more?

NANCY

(*Seemingly unaware of his embrace*)

I know why my grandfather likes it, and it may go for them too. He says it's the promised city that Southerners have never had and always craved. He says a big city should be a big country town, that when it gets to be anything else it's foreign to him, that it isn't "truly American any longer."

JIM

(*Still fondling*)

And what is it you crave, honey?

60

NANCY

(*Pulling away from him*)
I crave everything that isn't a country town in Tennessee.

JIM

That's *me* . . . And what I crave is a Southern gal named Nancy.

NANCY

Well, that's not me, Jimmy boy. If I don't teach you anything else, I'll teach you that a Southern girl is no different from other girls.

JIM

Last night you taught me just how different a Southern girl is.

NANCY

Kiss my foot.

JIM

Oh, come on, Nancy. I'm really keen on you. But I want to know if you were just kidding around.

NANCY

Stop saying, "just kidding around," Jim. There is something I want to know too . . . Why haven't you gone back to Princeton? Your mother said this morning you were due back two days ago . . . You get away with murder with your father and mother, don't you? (JIM *stands smoking, staring thoughtfully at* NANCY. NANCY *comes to him and puts her hand on his arm affectionately.*)

NANCY

Jim, tell me.

JIM

My parents tempt you to get away with murder. We have never had to do *anything*—Lanny and I—that we didn't want to do. They've always *trusted* us . . . and laughed at any idea that we would do something we shouldn't.

NANCY

That sounds to me the way parents ought to be.

JIM

Yeah . . . yeah. Only, that's not quite the whole picture. They don't like to think that anything could go wrong for anybody in this family. They *won't* think it. They assume that if I don't go back to college on time after the holidays, it must be all right. They haven't asked me a direct question about why I haven't gone back. They don't want to know why. They feel that if they had to ask me why, it would be the same as admitting something *might* be wrong.

NANCY

Why *haven't* you gone?

JIM

Reasons, chile. Good reasons.

NANCY

I think I know why.

JIM

Ha!

NANCY

I had some talk with Lanny in the car this morning, when we were waiting for your mother once.

JIM

A lot he knows.

NANCY

He knows that you and your Uncle William have been having long bull sessions every day or so since you came for Christmas. He thinks you two have some kind of scheme up.

JIM

Oh, he does?

NANCY

Jim, I want to go with you!

JIM

You what? Quit the kidding.

NANCY

So it was you who wasn't sincere last night?

JIM

That brat brother of mine has gotten things mixed up, Nancy. Or you have. I'm not going anywhere. Not anywhere. Not even back to Princeton. I've flunked out. It's Uncle Brother, Uncle

63

William who is leaving. I've been trying to get him to take me with him, but he's not taking Lucy or anybody.

NANCY

So you are going to stay in St. Louis.

JIM

Yeah . . . yeah. (*Heavily ironic*) I'll stay here and get married . . . and have three swell kids . . . and go down hill fast as hell. That's what Princeton men do in St. Louis.

NANCY

(*Laughing*)

Oh, Jim, you're priceless. (*Snuggling to him*) Jim, where do you *think* he's going?

JIM

Oh, South America. Or maybe Europe to get mixed up in the war they're going to have, somehow. He won't tell me a damned thing about it. He just tortures me by saying he's found something new under the sun. By God, I wish I could make him take me with him, Nancy. He used to think I was all right, but he's turned against me somehow.

NANCY

Why do you have to go with *him*?

JIM

Because he'll do things in a big way. He's got all kinds of money. Do you know what he did this morning? He drew all the money he's put away in the past ten years out of the bank.

NANCY

You mean drew it out in cash?

JIM

I don't know, but he has two new traveling bags up in his room. Father says he's worth half a million.

NANCY

All that money in *this* house, right now?

JIM

I don't know. I guess not. But I know he drew out all his money this morning. He doesn't have any stocks or bonds or anything.

NANCY

He told you so? He told you he had drawn out his money?

JIM

No, I was with Father at the Bank when someone came in and told him. Uncle Brother was one of the really big depositors, and so Father almost *had* to know it. Besides, I'm sure Uncle Brother wanted him to. With all the banks there are in this town, he has never banked anywhere but at Father's bank, and all the time living here—right through the depression— and not paying a cent ... Father and Mother make people want to do things like that to them.

NANCY

When are you going to tell them you've flunked out of Princeton?

JIM

Never. When I've hung around here a little longer they'll realize I'm not going back. They won't say anything; they'll just quit referring to it. That's how they are. After a while I'll get a job, and, Nancy . . . I want us to get married.

NANCY

(*Lightly*)

Ha! Jimmy, we only met last night. You don't know me at all.

JIM

But I'm head over heels, Nancy, my gal, I really am.

(*They kiss as* WILLIAM *enters from left.*)

WILLIAM

Oho! So that's how it goes.

(NANCY *pulls away from* JIM *and slaps him.*)

JIM

Gad, Nancy, you didn't have to do that. It's only Uncle Brother.

(WILLIAM *crosses the room, whistling "Dixie," and fills his pipe from the tobacco jar on the table.*)

WILLIAM

You better go somewhere and get that lipstick off your face, Jim. I think the Senator's on his last anecdote. They'll all be in here in a minute. Your mother's got us scheduled for a game of keno.

(*Exit* JIM, *center.* WILLIAM *whistles another bar of* "Dixie," *still filling his pipe.*)

NANCY

Is that tune for my benefit?

WILLIAM

Was that slap for my benefit? Or was it the real McCoy?

NANCY

It was both . . .

WILLIAM

Mmmmmmmmmm.

NANCY

Since you're smoking their tobacco, how about finding me one of their cigarettes?

WILLIAM

What makes you think it's not my tobacco?

NANCY

It's not your house, is it?

WILLIAM
(*Yawning*)

No, but I live here.

NANCY

Why?

WILLIAM

It's convenient. It's my club.

NANCY

I hear you're very rich.

WILLIAM

(*Taking a cigarette from the box on the table*)
And greatly loved.

NANCY

Why don't you have a place of your own?

WILLIAM

I like living in a big house like this, but I wouldn't be caught owning it. It doesn't pay to own real estate like this. It's out of date to try to own things like this.
(*He puts the cigarette in her mouth.*)

NANCY

It's surely not my idea of the latest thing.

WILLIAM

No? . . . (*Lighting her cigarette*) How did you happen to come along on this trip with your granddaddy, Miss Nancy?

NANCY

(*Coyly*)
I had to get out of town.

WILLIAM

I can almost believe that.

NANCY

(*Seriously*)

Do you know what it is like to have to get away? To not be able to stand it any longer?

WILLIAM

(*After a silence*)

I hadn't really noticed you before, Nancy.

NANCY

I noticed you, William, right away.

WILLIAM

So that's how it goes, eh?

NANCY

So that's how it goes.

WILLIAM

You came along with the Senator just for the ride. For a change of scenery.

NANCY

When Granddaddy goes back home, I'm not going with him.

WILLIAM

You mean *you're* going to move in on them here, too?

NANCY

No ... I'm going with you.

WILLIAM

(*Angrily*)

What's that?

(*He begins to laugh aloud. Enter all others but* JIM, *from left.* NANCY's *back is to them. She watches* WILLIAM *with a serious expression until the others come forward enough to see her face. Then she bursts into laughter. Her laughter continues after* WILLIAM's *has stopped.*)

JAMES

What's the joke, William?

AUNTIE BET

When did William ever laugh at a *joke?*

HELEN

(*As* AUNTIE BET *and* FLO DEAR *move toward center exit*)
The keno game has to start soon, Auntie Bet, if—

AUNTIE BET

Oh, we'll be right back. Flo Dear and I are just going to freshen up a bit. Don't start without us.

(*Exeunt* AUNTIE BET *and* FLO DEAR.)

SENATOR CASWELL

It was a glorious meal, Helen.

HELEN

I am glad you enjoyed it, Cousin Cameron.

70

SENATOR CASWELL

I enjoyed it enormously ... enormously.

HELEN

Who's game for a round of darts?

LANNY

I am.

HELEN

No, you're going to finish that crossword puzzle for me, Lan.
I put it with your book there on the table.
> (LANNY *picks up the book and the puzzle and sits down,
> far right and back.*)

JAMES

I suppose I'll have to be your victim. Just one round each. And
yours first.

LUCY

Ah, we're going to have an exhibition, Senator. But Helen
will win. She's the champion.
> (HELEN *throws.*)

WILLIAM

The sacrifice of the male animal. I don't believe in it.

NANCY

That had a nasty ring.
> (*All watch* HELEN. *The small target is hung on the wall,
> near the left corner of the room.*)

WILLIAM

If so, it will be lost on them. They're the eternal sweethearts. Their motto is: Life must *seem* beautiful.

HELEN

(*As she throws*)

Your life too can seem beautiful, William. Just follow the simple directions.

(*Enter* JIM, *center.*)

WILLIAM

(*Pointing with thumb*)

Yes, speak-no-evil and see-no-evil. That's what I call them.

NANCY

Then you ought to call Granddaddy, hear-no-evil.

(JIM *sits down at ping-pong table, facing the audience, beside* NANCY. *The table is downstage, right. During the talk above* LUCY *has removed the ping-pong net and pulled up several straight chairs.* LUCY *has sat down at right end of table,* WILLIAM *at left end,* NANCY *at* WIL-LIAM's *left.*)

JIM

Well, when does this game of keno begin, Mother?

HELEN

Bull's-eye! A hundred and fifty points. I've got him licked.

SENATOR CASWELL

(*Downstage left*)

Looks as though the lady will be the winner.

JIM

She's always the winner. Why else do you think she's forever organizing games? (*In good humor*) So she can lord it over us all.

JAMES

He speaks for himself, Senator. And for Lanny. Not for me. I have my turn now. Watch!
(*He throws.*)

HELEN

Ah, that won't hurt me. Twenty-five points.
(JAMES *throws again, and continues till he has thrown all six darts.*)

SENATOR CASWELL
(*In a loud voice*)
Is it skill or luck she has?

WILLIAM

It's some of both. She and James are two of the luckiest people you'll ever meet.

SENATOR CASWELL
(*Meaningfully*)
I can see that they are.

WILLIAM

In games I mean, of course . . . (*To* NANCY) He is a match for her in most things, but neither of these boys can stand up to her in any game. I've seen her whip them in chess, checkers, bridge, poker—that's her real game—and even horseshoes.

73

JAMES

There! That did it . . . or almost. Three hundred and fifty, four twenty-five . . .

HELEN

No, it's my score. Nine twenty-five to nine hundred. Give me a quarter. But you were wonderful.

JAMES

No, you were wonderful!

LANNY

(*Upstage right, deep in chair with book, hardly visible to audience*)

Listen to them.

HELEN

Now let's get on with a rousing game of keno. Everybody in.

LANNY

No, I'm not playing.

WILLIAM

(*To* NANCY)

In the summertime it's even worse. James and Helen are as brown as shoe leather from golf, and the rest of us are as white as sheets. Jim *tries* to play golf with them; he's just no good.

JIM

Nancy doesn't like games any better than the rest of us.

LANNY

The trouble with Mother and Father is that they have nothing in common but games. They have to play games to keep from boring each other to death.

HELEN

(*Coming forward*)

These are my jewels. My adoring children. Now for some keno. How's the crossword puzzle going, Lanny?

JIM

(*To* NANCY)

While she played one game with Father she had us waiting to play another, and she had Lanny at work on a puzzle!

HELEN

What's the hurry, Jim? We have the whole afternoon before us. (*Gesturing grandly*) You have all of life before you.

JIM

Nancy and I are going to a party at five.

NANCY

A tea dance, no less.

HELEN

That's the kind of life my children lead. Teas, dinners, and dances!

JIM

Furthermore, Nancy wants to borrow an old dress of yours to wear. It's a twenties party.

75

WILLIAM

A twenties party? That's one I haven't heard.

NANCY

Yes, everyone dresses in clothes from the twenties.
(WILLIAM *sits looking at* NANCY, *as though stunned*.)

LUCY

Look at the dour expression on William's face.

HELEN

He's older than he thinks . . . But don't let your mind dwell on it, Brother. You'll be having another of your nightmares tonight.

LUCY

Twenties parties are taking the place of gay nineties parties, William.

NANCY

The twenties must have been a swell time to grow up. The trouble with growing up in the thirties is that there will be nothing to remember, not even anything to make fun of . . . Life in the twenties must have been exciting.

LUCY

Oh, it was, wasn't it, Uncle William?

JIM

Where are the cards? And where are the keno boards? Mother insists that we all play keno—grown people sitting around on a Saturday afternoon playing keno—and yet she keeps us waiting for fifteen minutes and hasn't even got the boards out yet.

HELEN

(*With feigned indifference*)
The cards and the boards are in the closet.

JIM

Aha! But for some reason the closet door is locked. I *wonder* why!

JAMES

I'll get them. (*Sotto voce*) You've said enough, Jim.
(*He hurries to the closet and fetches the boards and cards.*)

JIM

Oh, she's a foxy one. I can tell by her manner she has already tried the door. What do you suppose is in there? A surprise for someone? For some special occasion?

HELEN

(*Sotto voce*)
We're not mentioning occasions, Jim. Change the subject. Be your age.

WILLIAM

(*To* NANCY)
It must be the family skeleton they have in the closet.

HELEN

Cousin Cameron, I don't know what to make of my son Jim. (*Walks toward the* SENATOR) After years of being what we thought was the silent type—emulating his uncle here—he has suddenly become talkative, and brilliantly so. His words are full of wit and irony and charm. I can't understand it. Do you suppose it could be your granddaughter who's bringing out this side of him?

JIM

Now who's being childish?

NANCY

Granddaddy's dozing.

SENATOR CASWELL

Who says I'm dozing? ... Yes, he is a handsome boy, Helen. He has a very cultured voice.

HELEN

Oh, very much the Princeton type. He was supposed to be back at Princeton two days ago. He must have had a premonition about Nancy. (*Turning toward the ping-pong table again*) Yes, he's very handsome, like his father.

WILLIAM

(*From the corner of his mouth*)
I'm leaving. They're just going to talk.

LUCY

Be patient, William. Besides, whenever wasn't their talk more fun than keno?

JAMES

(*Distributing the boards*)

He gets his good looks from you, my dear.

LANNY

(*Aloud*)

Listen to them. The owl and the pussy cat.

HELEN

No, it's from me he inherits his gift for language.

JIM

The game, Mother! We are here to play keno! (*To* NANCY)
It's like this every Saturday afternoon.

NANCY

I think they're grand.

JIM

This game business finally gets on your nerves. But it'll be
worse if they get to talking about their childhood or about
characters they used to know in Tennessee ... They don't know
what reality is.

(WILLIAM *laughs scornfully, quietly.*)

LUCY

Why do you laugh at Jim? It is something you might say
yourself.

WILLIAM

(*Leaning forward*)

It's something I *have* said. Jim's a parrrot. Gets to be more of
one every day.

HELEN

(*At ping-pong table, but still standing*)

Stop this muttering in the ranks! The game *can't* begin until
Auntie Bet and Flo Dear come down. And remember all bets
are strictly *sub rosa* as long as Flo Dear is present. Everybody
make his arrangements about betting now . . . Brother and I
have a permanent quarter on the corner arrangement. But no
mention of it after Flo Dear comes down.

JIM

(*To* NANCY)

Think of that. Everything in this house has to go according
to some notion of Flo Dear's or Auntie Bet's.

JAMES

(*To* LANNY, *who has refused the keno card offered him*)

Lanny, if you are not going to play, why don't you go in the
library or upstairs to finish your puzzle. Don't be a kill-joy.

LANNY

I've finished the puzzle, Father. And I am not being a kill-
joy.

JIM

(*Pointing to* LANNY)

He's really batty, you know. Look at him. He thinks he's
Napoleon on . . . Mount Everest.

LANNY

I suppose you mean St. Helena, Jim.

JIM

Who cares.

LANNY

(*Standing*)

Nobody cares. "I felt my isolation. And so, on all sides I let down anchors of safety to the bottom of the sea."

JAMES

Go along, son. You heard what I said.

LANNY

Do I have to disappear off the face of the earth just because I want to read? I'm reading the life of Sam Davis.

JIM

Who cares what you're reading?

JAMES

Hush, Jim.

LANNY

Jim doesn't know who Sam Davis was.

JIM

And couldn't care less.

LANNY

He was the boy-hero of the Confederacy and was hanged for spying, near Nashville.

81

JIM

Oh, God, I *can* care less even than I thought I could.

HELEN

Now he is being himself, Nancy. This is what he's really like. What's become of all that urbanity now?

LANNY

(*Laughing*)

Urbanity!

JIM

(*Turning around quickly in his chair*)

Listen, Lanny—

JAMES

I said for you two to stop this bickering. You're grown men!

HELEN

You see how much control my husband has over the boys, Cousin Cameron. It's because he has never beaten them. If I were their father, oh, boy, I'd make them step. But I am only their gentle little mother to whom they must be free to turn in time of trouble.

LANNY

She lashes us with her tongue.

SENATOR CASWELL

(*Clearing his throat*)

It has always been difficult for me to understand the objection that people make to gambling.

NANCY

(*Sotto voce*)

This is one of his favorite themes. We *will* be here all afternoon.

LANNY

(*Straightening in his chair, craning his neck*)

Cousin Cameron, it is because Flo Dear was born a Methodist. She feels—

WILLIAM

(*Booming interruption*)

Gambling, Senator . . . gambling doesn't appeal to people (*Rising*) who have real self-confidence or to people who know— or think they know—what life is worth to them.

(LANNY *starts to leave the room.*)

JAMES

Where are you going, Lanny?

LANNY

(*Bitterly*)

I was trying to say something. Didn't you hear Uncle William interrupt me?

JAMES

You had better stay.

HELEN

For heaven's sake, let him go, James. (*To* LANNY) If you must go, go and see what's keeping Auntie Bet and Flo Dear. Tell them the keno game is waiting on them.

(*Exit* LANNY, *center.*)

SENATOR CASWELL

I am not certain that I understand you, sir, but I suspect that I heartily disagree with what you said.

WILLIAM

I mean that the men I have known who have gambled for a living have been nervous, senseless sort of men.

SENATOR CASWELL

Oh?

WILLIAM

They haven't had sense enough to know what they want or to know that there's nothing they want. All they know is that they have nothing and they ought to want something.

HELEN

Everyone's talking brilliantly today.

WILLIAM

On the other hand, people who do a lot of little gambling without really risking anything are people who feel that they *have* everything. Maybe they just like to tease themselves and to play that at any moment they might lose everything. Like the real gamblers, they're bored.

JAMES

One can see you have given this a lot of thought, William.

HELEN

(Sitting down at table)

Brother, if this is supposed to be an insult to *me,* it is like water on a duck's back, I assure you.

(JIM *gets up and goes toward* WILLIAM.)

SENATOR CASWELL

He makes gamblers sound mighty mysterious and fascinatin' ... I don't know what gambling means to the people in those extreme circumstances he speaks of. He seems to know. I don't ... I'll say, though, that almost any trifling little game of chance seems to me like a small abstraction of life itself—so much so that it seems almost a sacred thing. For that reason I have always regarded professional gamblers much as I do preachers and priests of all kinds.

JAMES

I wonder if any of you ever heard of old Captain Bobby Bennett down at Memphis? He was an old-time river gambler, so they used to say.

(JIM *stands shaking his head.*)

HELEN

Oh, James, what a coincidence. I was just remembering stories that Papa used to tell about Captain Bobby.

WILLIAM

Yes, Papa knew him. But Papa never knew him the way I did. I played poker with him a couple of times in the old Gayoso Hotel at Memphis, when he was ninety and almost blind.

HELEN

Did you, Brother? Did Papa know it?

WILLIAM

If Papa knew it, he rolled over in his grave. The fact is it was right after Papa died; I was just a youngster, and when old Bobby found out how young I was he wouldn't let me get in the games any more.

SENATOR CASWELL

Did Bobby Bennett impress you, then, as a nervous, senseless sort of man?

WILLIAM

No, Senator, he did not. But he was of an older generation, and it would have been harder for me to know what he was really like. He was a gentleman, in the old-time sense of the word, though.

SENATOR CASWELL

Yes, he was a tidewater gentleman. There was nothing up-country about him. But a lot of the old-time gamblers were like that. *He* wasn't nearly the gentleman that John Lacey Warfield was.

LUCY

Oh, John Lacey Warfield! That's one that I've heard of.

HELEN

Surely *every*one's heard of John Lacey Warfield.

JIM

(*To* NANCY)

Oh, everyone!

SENATOR CASWELL

Bobby Bennett was Lilliputian compared to John Lacey War-field and to others who went even before John Lacey Warfield. There was Miles Murphy, who rode with old Forrest in '63. *There* was a dashing, reckless gentleman-gambler for you. *There* was a man to whom the standard rules of behavior did not apply.

LUCY

It's a pity Lanny isn't present to hear this.

SENATOR CASWELL

It was said that in his early years Miles Murphy had a wife every fifty miles along the Natchez Trace, and in his middle years he had them scattered along the Mississippi, and in his old age he had a devoted family at every whistle stop along the I. C. . . . But in a game of cards he was ever the soul of honor.

JAMES

How about Jesse Hayne and Colonel McKinney? They were famous.

SENATOR CASWELL

Yes, they *were* famous in their day. But I didn't know you would even have heard of them, James. Of course back in Jackson's day—a hundred years ago when Jackson was swapping horses with Wade Hampton in South Carolina—they were all gentleman-gamblers. They felt that gambling was good for the soul ... You see, in a good gambling game a man tests equally his skill and his luck. (NANCY *groans*) And, why, those are the things a man's wanting to know the answer to every day of his life: how skillful is he and what is his luck? Skill's a great thing, but it's no good without luck. It would be a dull—no, a terrifying life if skill were everything. Luck is the most marvelous thing in the world, and no man knows whether or not he is lucky till he's seen his last day.

JIM

Have you been lucky, Cousin Cameron?

SENATOR CASWELL

(*Still addressing* WILLIAM)

In old-time politics we used to say you must always fight the hardest campaign you can, but on the night of the election when they're counting the votes and you sit in the smoke-filled hotel room with your friends, nobody's thinking of anything but his luck. It's like the hours before death, I reckon. And you know that the outcome depends not on the skill or lack of skill you've shown in the campaign but on what side your old daddy took in the War Between the States, on a thousand other things, on how people got out of their beds that morning, on how the corn and tobacco and the cotton are doing that year, on the color of hair you were born with, on the kind of voice you have—whether there's too much molasses in it or maybe too much mountain twang—

WILLIAM

(*With feeling*)

No! I won't admit that.

SENATOR CASWELL

Yes, it is so. Campaign all you will, the outcome of an election depends on things too diverse to consider. Everything from the conversion of St. Paul to the defeat of Prince Charlie counts for or against you in one way or another. Everything from the price of rice in China to the price of shoes in St. Louis. How these things fall together for you constitutes your luck.

WILLIAM

(*Laughing with great derision*)

There you have it in a nutshell, my friends. (*In a very loud voice*) That's how the world goes. (*Thumping* JIM *on the chest*) Remember that, young man!

(*Laughing again, he walks toward the ping-pong table.*)

JAMES

William, there is no cause for such rudeness.

WILLIAM

(*Very loud*)

Ho, ho, ho.

LUCY

Well, I'm glad Lanny's not present for this.

HELEN

Do stop Brother, Lucy.

LUCY

You stop him, Helen. He's *your* brother.

JIM

(*Returning to table, to* NANCY)
What is everybody getting so excited about?

NANCY

Just look at Granddaddy. He's only begun.

SENATOR CASWELL

(*Untouched by* WILLIAM's *laughter, deaf to* JAMES *and* HELEN)
You moderns ... (*Approaching* WILLIAM *at table*) You moderns think only of skill. We old-timers thought of our luck too. We were superstitious about it.

LUCY

To me, it is you who sounds modern, Senator. And from me that's a compliment. It is William who is really old-fashioned in his view of things.

JIM

Can't we change the subject? There is always keno!
(*He holds up the board.*)

WILLIAM

Senator, you know what you are talking about, all right, when you say what determines somebody's luck. It *is* politics and history and the kind of people you happen to be born into and where and when and with how much money. All that is what people call luck, all right. And you seem to like it. But I am not interested in being a political animal or an economic animal or even the son of my time. To hell with it.

SENATOR CASWELL

My cousin, you have no sense of history.
(*He turns his back.*)

WILLIAM

You can have history. The trick is to operate outside history.
The only interest anybody should have in past history should
be for the purpose of better exploiting present history.
(FLO DEAR *enters hurriedly on tiptoe, going directly to*
HELEN.)

LUCY

"If drunk with sight of power we loose
Wild tongues that have not Thee in awe
Be with us yet. Be with us yet."

FLO DEAR

(*Sotto voce*)

Come upstairs quickly, Helen.

HELEN

What is it?

FLO DEAR

Betty's not well. She needs you . . . and James. It's her heart,
I think.
(*They move quickly to* JAMES.)

SENATOR CASWELL

"Such boastings as the Gentiles use
Or lesser breeds without the law."

JIM

We used to sing that in school, and there was a fellow named Lesser in my class. I thought it was about him—"Lesser breed without the law"—or his father.

JAMES

(*Sotto voce*)

Maybe it's indigestion. Have you called Dr. Wallace?

FLO DEAR

No ... (*Agitated*) Oh, I don't know.
  (*Exit* JAMES, *followed by* FLO DEAR. HELEN *goes to* LUCY, *who stands up.*)

SENATOR CASWELL

Jim, when Nancy was a little mite about so high we overheard her singing the old Sunday School song:

"When your life rings true, when your life rings true,
There will be a nickel coming back to you."

HELEN

(*To* LUCY)

Auntie Bet's had some kind of upset. Try to keep things going. No need for Cousin Cameron to know.

LUCY

I hope it's nothing serious.

HELEN

Flo Dear thinks it's her heart. I doubt it.

NANCY

That wasn't me, Granddaddy. It was one of your other grandchildren.

SENATOR CASWELL

It may not have been you who said *that,* my dear, but it was you who came to me at the age of five and asked to touch my bald head ... And when she put her little finger on it, she asked, "Does it hurt, Granddaddy?"

> (*Exit* HELEN *during the above speech. A moment during which the sound of the clock can be distinguished faintly.*)

SENATOR CASWELL

(*Looking toward doorway*)

They are grand people, Helen and James. I hope Miss Betty is not seriously ill.

NANCY

He always hears whatever you don't want him to.

WILLIAM

(*To* LUCY)

Is this heart attack business a ruse to keep me from pulling out?

LUCY

(*Sotto voce*)

If it is a ruse at all, it is to draw off some of the attention the Senator's basking in ... (*Aloud*) Senator, I don't imagine Miss Betty's very sick. She's more given to indigestion than to heart trouble.

93

SENATOR CASWELL

(*Concerned*)

She is a very remarkable lady. A person of real feeling and courage.

WILLIAM

(*Laughing*)

On what do you base that judgment, Senator?

SENATOR CASWELL

On the circumstances of her departure from Nashville some twelve or fourteen years ago.

NANCY

Gracious God! You knew Miss Betty in Nashville, Granddaddy?

SENATOR CASWELL

No, but I knew her story well. You could not be in Nashville at the time without knowing it, and that happened to be during my last term in office as Governor. If ever Nashville had a social arbiter, it was Miss Betty Pettigru. (*Everyone is spellbound*) And apparently it was not a position she was born into. She came to Nashville, already an old maid by the standards of the time, from out at the country town of Thornton, and then over a period of years she attained her ascendancy through perseverance and, according to the story, only after many cruel insults and setbacks and after learning, herself, to be somewhat ruthless.

WILLIAM

(*Laughing*)

You call that courage, Senator?

94

SENATOR CASWELL

Courage of a sort, sir. (*Smiling*) A kind of animal courage. The courage of a warrior. But that's not the courage I was speaking of. When Miss Betty was a woman of almost sixty and at the height of her power, she abruptly left the scene of her victories and came off to St. Louis to live with distant relatives who set little store by the things she had foolishly given her life to. People in Nashville could hardly believe it at first. They said it was the most momentous event and the greatest mystery since Sam Houston deserted his new bride and the Governor's chair and went to Texas. Nobody could understand it and nobody believed the reason she gave: that she had lost her heart to the two small sons of her cousins here and wanted only to be near them. But it was true. I had half forgotten the story until last year when I heard that this was the family Miss Betty and her cousin Miss Flo had come to live with. Suddenly Miss Betty's story held an irresistible fascination for me . . . just because it contrasted with the story of my first coming here.

NANCY

Yes, Granddaddy, it is well known you came here to get away from the reality of family life, not to find it.

SENATOR CASWELL

(*Genuinely shocked*)

From your lips, Nancy? . . . The voice of your mother, and your mother's mother, and your . . . and my own mother.

(*Pause.*)

WILLIAM

(Rising, as though somewhat shocked himself by the SENATOR,
a suggestion of sympathy in his voice)

Senator . . . Senator Caswell . . . What a damned crazy
thought I have had—about you and me. Sir, why did you ever
start coming here . . . to St. Louis?

SENATOR CASWELL

Why? Or how? Well, it's all one. It was by purest chance,
you see, though possibly it could not have happened to anyone—
to any man—except a Southerner of my generation. I picked
up a pamphlet—an advertisement—in a Pullman seat, on a train
going through West Virginia. It was something got out by a
man in St. Louis named Lemoin Bradford advertising fire insurance. How it got there, who can say? Pure chance. But I had
had an old cousin by that name who went out to the Panhandle
back in the eighties, and it struck me that this might be his son
or grandson. And, you know, it was! I wrote him, and it wasn't
six months before I was here visiting him and his sister, an old
bachelor and an old maid. They are the children of Cousin
Lemoin Bradford! They live in a little apartment near here
somewhere, I think—on Pershing Street. Everyone they knew
was from Tennessee or Kentucky—their grocer, their laundry-
man, their one servant. They were sentimental about the region,
though neither Lemoin or his sister had ever been there.
Through them I began meeting all these Southern people. It
has been a wonderful experience, I tell you.

WILLIAM

But why? Why has it?

SENATOR CASWELL

How can I say why? How can I really put it into words?
(*He turns his back and walks farther downstage left.*
WILLIAM *follows him a few steps. Enter* FLO DEAR *center,*
out of breath.)

FLO DEAR

William! Jim! Go quickly upstairs! (*Sitting down on straight*
chair near doorway, panting) They need you to force the door!

WILLIAM

Where? Where, Flo?

FLO DEAR

To Lanny's room.
(*Exeunt* WILLIAM *and* JIM, *center.* FLO DEAR *starts to get*
up, but LUCY *comes to her and puts her hand on her*
shoulder. SENATOR CASWELL *stands facing the audience,*
downstage left.)

LUCY

No, Flo, wait a moment. You mustn't climb those stairs
again. *You*'ll be having a heart attack. What is it about Lanny's
room?

FLO DEAR

(*In a hoarse voice*)
It isn't Betty. It was her idea I should say that, so the Senator
wouldn't know. It's little Lanny. When we went up after lunch
Betty noticed her pills were gone—her sleeping pills . . . We
looked and looked, and then when Lanny came up a while ago

97

Betty told him. He seemed a little queer and presently he went across the hall to his room and shut the door. I don't know which of us suspected first, but we rushed over there right away, and he wouldn't let us in.

(*There has been the distant sound of the men forcing the door, but now only the clock.*)

NANCY

The poor, dumb, little idiot.

LUCY

(*To* FLO DEAR)

Getting to him this quickly they can make him vomit it all. He'll be all right in no time.

FLO DEAR

But to think how unhappy he must have been to do such a thing. What could it be?

LUCY

(*Rushing out*)

Oh, Lanny!

SENATOR CASWELL

(*Turning around, hesitantly*)

One of the boys ... is ill?

FLO DEAR

(*Standing and speaking in a loud voice,
as though to a deaf person*)

He's going to be all right, Senator, I am sure.

SENATOR CASWELL

Splendid. Splendid.

NANCY

(*Sotto voce*)

Yes, splendid. Oh, God.

Curtain

ACT
THREE

ACT THREE

The game room. Six in the evening. No light except a faint one coming from the hallway through the center door. Only a glow from the fireplace. The room seems empty. The clock on the mantel ticks away. Enter LUCY, *center. She pauses in the doorway, then steps forward and switches on table lamp beside the door. She moves slowly across the dimly-lit room toward the fireplace. She stands gazing into the fire for a moment, then opens the glass door of the clock and stops the pendulum. Dead silence.* WILLIAM *is seated in the big chair* LANNY *sat in during the second act, upstage right. When he speaks it is in a deep, startled whisper.*

WILLIAM

Lucy!

LUCY

(*A stifled scream, then*)
Christ! William! . . . How cruel of you to frighten me.

WILLIAM

(*Rising from chair*)
It's you, Lucy? I thought it was Helen.

LUCY

Then why did you call my name?

WILLIAM

Did I call your name? . . . Oh, it was something I was dreaming. I was asleep there.

LUCY

Only you could sleep at such a time, William.

WILLIAM

(*Shaking his head*)

God, for a minute I wasn't sure I had been asleep. You weren't you in the dream really. Or I wasn't me. Something like that. And then I woke up and thought you were Helen, over there.

LUCY

It's Helen's dress I'm wearing.

WILLIAM

(*Incredulous*)

You're going to the banquet, Lucy?

LUCY

I am. I suppose that's the final step in my degradation. (*Silence.*)

WILLIAM

How's Lanny by now? Oh, he was in it too! (LUCY *looks at him, not understanding*) . . . The dream.

LUCY

Lanny's been quieter than usual, but that's all. He's O.K. He's up in his room, reading.

WILLIAM

No reasons given? No excuses?

LUCY

None. He's coming downstairs to supper. I'd go out to eat if I were you. Only he and Helen will be here.

WILLIAM

You're going to the banquet in Sister's place, I take it . . . It's not often I have a dream that seems so near to what's really going on. Usually I'm fighting Indians or gangsters.

LUCY

Yes, I am going to the banquet in Helen's place.

WILLIAM

(*Hesitantly*)

She's pretty much torn up still?

LUCY

Oh, Helen's Helen. She's in good shape. Nobody says so, but they are really sending me just to give me something to do this evening. Otherwise, it would seem logical for me to stay here with Lanny. *That* wouldn't be a good idea. He doesn't need a confidante tonight.

WILLIAM

No, I guess he doesn't . . . It hardly seems possible.

LUCY

What does?

WILLIAM

That that boy's up . . . eating . . . and . . . reading. What a
hell of a half hour it was this afternoon! It doesn't seem real now.
Why, what I just dreamed seems more real. Lucy, while I was
asleep just now—

LUCY

I haven't congratulated you, have I? Without you, Lanny
might not be alive now.

WILLIAM

There wasn't any danger of his not being alive. The pills had
hardly gotten to his stomach. Dr. Wallace would have rushed
him to a hospital.

LUCY

Yes, when Dr. Wallace finally got here. Anyway, without
you Lanny would have had the stomach pump and the hospital,
and the newspapers. Really, though, I don't think it was anything you did that made him vomit; I think it was the fear or
the anger he felt with you holding him and talking to him like
that. But however it was, I thank you. (*Bitterly*) I thank you,
William, from the bottom of my heart for saving that boy, for
saving him just the least bit of suffering and humiliation.

    (WILLIAM *suddenly sits down in a chair nearer to* LUCY
    *than before, and hides his face in his hands. Seeing him
    do so,* LUCY *abruptly turns her back to him, covering her
    own face and weeping.*)

LUCY

Don't, William. Don't give an inch.

WILLIAM

(*Removing his hands*)

Don't give an inch?

LUCY

No, for God's sake. If nothing else, go on to the end being you. Don't be touched by this thing, don't be *moved* by what happened today. I couldn't stand it. It would make your going away twice as hard for me.

WILLIAM

(*Seeming not to have heard her*)

Damn it . . . Damn it . . . I remember it all. I remember what I was dreaming over there. I thought I had decided not to go.

LUCY

And it was a nightmare?

WILLIAM

No, it wasn't a nightmare . . . Lucy, what if I didn't go?
(*Silence.*)

LUCY

People aren't really changed by things that happen to them, things like that half hour this afternoon. Not really. When people change, it's all physiological. I thought we agreed on that. The changes that you attribute to me would have taken place, no matter what, as I grew older.

WILLIAM

(*As if to himself*)

I dreamed we were set up in a house a good deal like this one.

LUCY

I couldn't stand it if you didn't go now. I wouldn't be up to it. William, I know too well the only way that you can be different from what you have been for the last ten years. I remember there's a side of your character that's weak as water, and I know there's no middle ground for you. I prefer you hard as rock.

WILLIAM

The water in my character may have dried up, Lucy. What if I didn't go away?

LUCY

I don't believe you are considering staying. Not for a moment.

WILLIAM

(*Flatly*)

It doesn't seem likely to you that I could be "touched" by anything that happened. In a way you're right. I wasn't touched just now by what you said about Lanny's suffering and humiliation. But when you mentioned my holding him, it came back to me how that boy felt when I was holding him—that's when I was touched—dragging him into the bathroom, squeezing his middle, dragging him back to his room again. It was how he felt to me that touched me. Poor, skinny, helpless kid. And yet he puts up a kind of fight against all of us. A kind I haven't ever put up.

LUCY

(*Stony*)

Yes, I was watching you when you finally let go of him. It was with a certain gentleness after all that roughness.

WILLIAM

Maybe I'm not really thinking of staying. But I could be a better father, mother, brother, aunt to Lanny than anyone here will ever be. My God, it was typical, their calling that old Dr. Wallace—just because he's from down home.

LUCY

(*Laughing a little*)

He was an hour getting here. And the only thing he said about Lanny was that he ought to have a good licking. He doesn't believe suicides should be saved from themselves . . . I do.

WILLIAM

Was Lanny really trying to do himself in, Lucy?

LUCY

Who ever can know? He will never know, himself.

WILLIAM

Lucy, could it have had anything to do with what I walked in on this morning, the thing between you and him? Did he know my plans?

LUCY

He suspected something was up. But it wasn't that. It *couldn't* have been.

WILLIAM

This is his damned birthday. Could it have been nobody's mentioning that? Did he just want attention? Is he that much of a kid?

LUCY

It wasn't that either—not about his birthday. Oh, it was everything. He was upset, and he was excited by the Senator's visit. He wanted the Senator's attention most terribly, and the old man seems to dislike him for no reason at all.

WILLIAM

The Senator's a queer one.

LUCY

He is that.

WILLIAM

Yet he's not half the fool—or not the kind of fool—I took him for. He and I had a talk here this afternoon after everybody was upstairs. He has, to say the least, some mixed feelings about his own family and about family things in general (*Laughing*) though he kept telling me how much I had missed. But he talks sense when you are alone with him. He has real intelligence, the way Lanny has . . . the way I haven't. Damn it, they can talk it out of their system. By God, it's easier for them.
  (*Silence.*)

LUCY

All right, what's easier, William?

WILLIAM

Oh, talk's easier . . . Anyhow, I told the old fellow he ought to have a session with Lanny, and he said he would.

LUCY

I'm glad of that, William. It's very important. It may make all the difference to Lanny in his excited state. Thank you.

WILLIAM

You're chock full of thanks about Lanny.

LUCY

Yes.

WILLIAM

We have ... "grown apart," haven't we?—you and me. But could it turn out, Lucy, that I've "matured" without your knowing it? Without even knowing it myself?

LUCY

You wouldn't be going away—

WILLIAM

What I dreamed was—I dreamed we had a boy just Lanny's age. We *could* have had, Lucy! The kid in my dream *was* actually Lanny, except of course he wasn't. (*Laughing*) He was threatening me somehow, and I was scared as hell of him. I called out to you.

LUCY

William, now it is *I* who can hardly believe *my* ears.

WILLIAM

I am only saying what I dreamed.

LUCY

(*Affecting to be bored*)
This feeling of yours will pass, William. Or if it doesn't, it won't concern me. It will concern, perhaps, someone like Nancy.
(WILLIAM *laughs*.)

111

LUCY

(*Angry*)

It's children you suddenly seem to want, isn't it? And I am too old to have children. And after tonight I won't even be mothering Lanny. I'll have no business coming here when you're gone—no excuse.

WILLIAM

(*Putting his arm about her, awkwardly but familiarly*)

I'm not thinking about having children of my own. That part of the dream *was* a nightmare. That's what woke me up. But I am thinking maybe about staying here and about our getting on a different footing somehow with Lanny and even Jim. Why, we might take Jim in the business and make a man out of him. And Lucy, you—

LUCY

It's a mirage you're seeing, William. Don't confuse your dreams with what's real. It's always been your peculiar strength that you didn't do that.

WILLIAM

It's not worth a try even? For you and me? You would be against it?

LUCY

It would have to have more thought from you than you have had time to give it.

WILLIAM

I'm going downtown now. I'll get a bite to eat somewhere and then go over to the office. I'll be there all evening. Sister is having a great herd of people here after the banquet. I'll be back before that's done with, and take you home . . . I leave it up to you, Lucy.

(*He kisses her. At this juncture* AUNTIE BET *wanders in, center, her eyes lowered as she brushes at her beaded evening dress, her fingers bedecked with rings.*)

AUNTIE BET
(*Looking up*)
Heavens!

WILLIAM
(*Laughing*)
Auntie Bet! . . . Good-bye, Lucy.

(*He crosses the room and exits right. Silence.* AUNTIE BET *stands in the doorway, obviously puzzled by what she has seen.*)

AUNTIE BET
I am sorry for blundering in that way, Miss McDougal.

(LUCY *shrugs her shoulders, smiling absently, her eyes still on the door that* WILLIAM *closed behind him.*)

AUNTIE BET
Please excuse me. And I thought for one moment you were Helen.

LUCY
Yes, the dress. It must have seemed odd.

AUNTIE BET
(*With significance*)
Except perhaps if they had been parting?

113

LUCY

You don't have to be indirect with me, Miss Betty.

AUNTIE BET

(*Walking slowly downstage*)

I should like to be very direct about one thing, my dear. I think it a mistake for you to go to the banquet in Helen's place. It will focus attention upon your . . . embarrassing relationship to this family.

LUCY

I didn't think you would approve, Miss Betty. But, generally speaking, you don't approve of me anyway.

AUNTIE BET

Miss McDougal, we don't really know each other.

LUCY

After ten years I am still Miss McDougal, William's secretary —and worse—to you.

AUNTIE BET

I am sure you understand why.

LUCY

Of course I understand. You and I come out of the same world, Miss Betty. I have known other "Auntie Bets." I understand.

AUNTIE BET

(*Turning quickly*)

And I, Miss McDougal—

LUCY

Yes, you have known other Lucy McDougals.

AUNTIE BET

I suppose it is a dark moment in life for you. But, generally speaking, aren't such moments inevitable for women who follow the course you have?

LUCY

The moment is not so dark as you imagine. It was not a parting scene you witnessed just now.

AUNTIE BET

William is not going away?

LUCY

If that were decided, I would have excused myself from this conversation.

AUNTIE BET

I am sorry to have forced it upon you. But I felt compelled to speak my mind.

(*She turns to go.*)

LUCY

Don't go yet, Miss Betty. It is a good moment for me to talk with someone who knows me only as a type. We can talk in a more general way; and that's what I need. We can talk about our pasts, Miss Betty!

AUNTIE BET

I am not a woman with a past, Miss McDougal.

LUCY

Ah, Miss Betty, I thought you were. Not a past like mine, of course, but I thought that before you came here you had had a successful career of a sort.

AUNTIE BET

A successful career does not always imply a "past."

LUCY

Does it not, Miss Betty? For a woman? Well, I don't know. But, anyway, the picture I had of you was that you had steered a pretty independent course, that you had managed, by hook or crook, to make something out of a life that might have been a pretty sad and pointless affair.

AUNTIE BET

It is an erroneous picture. Even if I had stayed home in the country, my life would not have been a "sad and pointless affair."

LUCY

Ah, Miss Betty, the life of an old maid in one of those country towns of ours! I know what it is like. It was my alternative too. But the course we took—you and I—was that of learning to live as men—you, like the men of your generation; I, more like those of my own. Instead of children and husband, we had our independence, and we learned to value it.

AUNTIE BET

Well, the resemblance ends there, I think.

LUCY

No, it goes one step beyond that. In your case—well, because James and Helen and their children seemed to offer you what you had never had, you gave up your independence and your career.

AUNTIE BET

I made certain sacrifices, but there have been great compensations.

LUCY

And in my case—*I* grew to love the Tollivers too, and it has caused me to make "certain sacrifices."

AUNTIE BET

I am afraid I don't follow you.

LUCY

I have ceased to share William's view of things. It has cost me *that*.

AUNTIE BET

He *is* abandoning you, then? But you just told me that that was not a farewell scene.

LUCY

He leaves it up to me.

AUNTIE BET

He offers to take you with him if you wish to go? But you don't wish to go.

LUCY

He "offers" to stay, if I wish it. It is to be my decision . . .
Well, that's all there is to it. I have told someone now. That was
what I needed. Why don't you go along now, Miss Betty. I
won't go to the banquet if it would embarrass you.

AUNTIE BET

(*Coming to* LUCY)

My dear girl, my dear Lucy.

LUCY

(*Amused*)

My dear girl? My dear Lucy?

AUNTIE BET

I am very happy for you, Lucy. Do come to the banquet.
Everything will be different now. This is what we have all
been hoping for.

LUCY

Are you sure of that? Do you think it would make so much
difference if—

AUNTIE BET

If you and William were to marry? It would make all the
difference in the world—to you, Lucy, and to everyone.

LUCY

(*Doubtfully*)

But I am not sure that William or I meant marriage. Perhaps
it would mean that. I don't know how it would work. Oh,
that's why I must try to think. Does anyone understand, really,

how much William hates all human ties that might be binding
upon him in any way? Have the rest of you realized that William's great satisfaction in living here has been the daily re-
minder that he *is* free of you all. Back home, Miss Betty, he
used to be forever going off somewhere to take one kind of
job or another, but always he came back. And he said he came
back because in other places he didn't enjoy his freedom the
way he did in the face of those who might be a threat to it.
That's why he was able to make a go of it here . . . And if he
goes away this time it will mean putting this lifelong quarrel—
this quarrel with all of us, this quarrel with himself—it will
mean putting it behind him.

AUNTIE BET

If he stays, doesn't he mean to put it behind him just as definitely? Even more definitely?

LUCY

Yes, but it will be like admitting he has been wrong all these
years.

AUNTIE BET

Oh, he *has* been wrong, Lucy.

LUCY

No, not altogether wrong. Even I could never admit that.
(*Silence.*)

AUNTIE BET

Lucy . . . you and I do come out of the same world. Listen,
Lucy McDougal: you must think of yourself first. This is your

chance for the kind of happiness without which your old age will truly be a "pretty sad and pointless affair." And it is William's chance too, whether he knows it or not.

LUCY

You mean our getting married? Or just his staying on here?

AUNTIE BET

I mean your getting married, and nothing less. My dear, you may think this sounds trite and vulgar, but you must play your cards as I have played mine.

LUCY

But what *are* my cards? That's what I want someone to tell me.

AUNTIE BET

That is something you must discover for yourself. But do you remember the maiden aunts and the widows in your family, those of your mother's and grandmother's generation. Do you remember how indispensable they managed to make themselves in the house of some near or distant relative?

LUCY

I remember how hard they worked looking after the children and the chickens, and even the cows and horses sometimes—just to have a roof over their heads.

AUNTIE BET

It wasn't just to have a roof over their heads, Lucy—not in all cases.

LUCY

It was to get for themselves just what you and I have felt the need of?

AUNTIE BET

Those women created the legend of family pride in the South. It is such women always who make the young people remember that blood is thicker than water . . . Take Flo Dear. Flo's not a bit of kin to us, really. She was only married to a distant relative of mine, and a black sheep he was, a worthless lout who deserted Flo in less than a year after he married her.

LUCY

Didn't he commit suicide, Miss Betty?

AUNTIE BET

Well, he left his hat on the river bank. Some interpreted it as suicide. Others took it only for his sign that he was not ever coming back to his mousy, bookish little wife.

LUCY

How primitive that sounds.

AUNTIE BET

Well, Flo was taken in to live with first one and then another of our kinspeople there in the country, and by listening to them she learned more of the family history than any one of them knew. She became a sort of authority to whom they all turned. Finally I saw that I needed her in Nashville. I was trying to establish my elegibility for the Colonial Dames, and I sent for her.

LUCY

Are you suggesting that I take up the study of heraldry?

AUNTIE BET

I am suggesting that you marry William.

LUCY

I want to be sure about all of this. I think I understand. But I want to be sure. How is it that Flo Dear's story relates to me?

AUNTIE BET

Flo Dear played her cards—the only cards she had to play. Flo, the trustworthy, incorruptible, little female relative, her head a storehouse of exact information about the family. That is an invaluable hand to hold in a big family connection, full of indispensable cards. And I held a fine hand too, Lucy. I, the wealthy, domineering old aunt who might change her will 'most any day of the week, broad-minded, worldly-wise even— even a trifle wicked in my machinations, but wanting awfully to be loved by everyone. As indispensable to the game as Flo Dear. As indispensable, almost, as Helen Tolliver herself.

LUCY

Helen? Even Helen?

AUNTIE BET

Helen, the beautiful mother and wife, the very ideal of womanhood. Oh, Helen holds the real trumps.

122

LUCY

I see. I see. And I am to become another aunt. But to whom is it we are indispensable?

AUNTIE BET

Why, to the menfolks, Lucy McDougal. To the menfolks. To their sense of manliness, to their feeling of security and power and superiority. They grow to need us as they need food, and—

LUCY

Stop, Miss Betty, in the name of decency! You have impressed me sufficiently. You must admit it is a very ugly picture.

AUNTIE BET

But a faithful one.

LUCY

Oh, not any more. That's the way the world was once for us, but not any longer. It has changed, or it is changing.

AUNTIE BET

But not fast enough for you and me, Lucy. In our different ways we have both tried living as men. And look where it has brought us. Lucy, I have never regretted a moment my coming here.

LUCY

But it was only a career in Nashville society that you sacrificed. I would be sacrificing William, a human being—though only a *man,* you might say.

AUNTIE BET

Let me tell you about a person whom *I* sacrificed, Lucy.

LUCY

A man in your life, after all, Miss Betty?

AUNTIE BET

No. It was no mere man. And it was not a person who had spent his life exploiting me, as William has you. It was an innocent old Negro woman. Her name was Vennie. James and Helen had brought her with them from Tennessee, and when I came here to live she resented my presence with all her soul. She told me to my face soon after I arrived: "I was here before you came, and I'll be here when you gone." Until I came, she had been more than just cook or nurse to the boys. She had been a sort of grandmother, and she had no intention of being replaced by me. She tried to turn the boys against me, and she tried to turn the other servants against me. You've seen the type.

LUCY

There's one in every family.

AUNTIE BET

Oh, she was artful, and she had a wonderful hold on the boys. I would be preparing to take them sometimes, say, to the amusement park, and when Flo and I were all dressed and ready to go, we'd find that the boys were in Vennie's apartment, down in the basement, and that she was baking them a cake or a pie in her own little kitchen. I would never call them away from her, and when they came up it would be too late for us to go out. Oh, and she could tell them stories—somehow

124

that was the worst part—stories about old times in Tennessee, about Tolliver Negroes and Tolliver white people going hunting together and saving each other's lives, about Vennie's dwarf brother who was the only person small enough to be let down a well to save one of the white children who had fallen in, and about an uncle of James' who found an old Negro man half frozen to death in the woods and brought him home on his back.

LUCY

Lanny and Jim would repeat it all to you, I suppose.

AUNTIE BET

They would repeat her stories to me expecting me to match them with stories of my own. But I couldn't do it. I had never learned to bake cakes or to tell stories to children; I had never had the chance.

LUCY

Vennie held the cards and knew how to play them?

AUNTIE BET

The struggle between Vennie and me went on for two years, but finally it was I who won out. You'll hardly believe what I stooped to. Flo Dear has never forgiven me. I don't want her to. With money I turned the other servants against Vennie. That is, I turned her against them. She had seen to it that they continued to treat me as a guest in the house instead of as a member of the family, always bringing my breakfast to my room, and things like that. But I had my one advantage, and I took it. This was at the bottom of the depression. I persuaded

James to let me pay the servants' wages until times should get better. After the second month I began increasing Bert's and Emmaline's wages without doing the same for Vennie. It had its effect.

LUCY

Perhaps you should stop there, Miss Betty.

AUNTIE BET

Vennie never mentioned the money, but she began making scenes with Helen and James about the most trivial things. If they were late for meals, or if there was company. Finally one night when there were guests for dinner and our talk delayed the progress of the meal, she burst into the dining room shouting, "Quit 'at talkin' and eat dem victuals. I don't know what time you got, but it's bedtime back whar I be.". . . I paid her off the next morning. She didn't want to stay. James put her on the afternoon train to Tennessee . . . Flo Dear never forgave me. (*Silence*) My story seems to have left you speechless, Lucy.

LUCY

Yes, but I'm not surprised at any of it, really. I'm only shocked by how well you understand it all. Such things don't seem so bad when people don't understand what they're doing.

AUNTIE BET

I did it for love. I did it because I needed the love of Lanny and Jim more than Vennie did. She had a whole raft of children and grandchildren back in Tennessee.

LUCY

And are you not afraid, Miss Betty, that I might somehow replace you if I married William?

AUNTIE BET

No. Your hand would be different. You would be the *young* aunt . . . their young rich aunt. For William is very rich. You would have your own house. You and William—married— would enlarge the connection. If anything, it would enhance mine and Flo Dear's position.

LUCY

Miss Betty, you *can't* have thought of all this just now, on the spur of the moment.

AUNTIE BET

No, the possibility had occurred to me long before this.

LUCY

All possibilities occur to you.
  (*Silence.*)

AUNTIE BET

But now it certainly must be time to leave for the banquet. I'm glad you're going along. I must stir the others up and get us started . . . Use your head, Lucy McDougal. Play the cards you've been dealt. They are all you have.
  (*Exit* AUNTIE BET.)

LUCY

(*After a moment, balefully*)
Oh, William, what a foolish dream you had. You mustn't stay in this house another night . . . Good-bye, William. Oh,

good-bye. (*She moves quickly to the clock, and glancing at her wrist watch, she adjusts the clock's minute hand and then sets the pendulum in motion. Voices call* LUCY *from offstage*) Yes, I'm coming.

    (*She goes out, center.*)

Curtain

ACT
FOUR

ACT FOUR

The game room. Ten-thirty that evening. Two table lamps provide the only light. HELEN *is playing solitaire at a card table, left. The great sliding doors, center, are closed. Presently* BERT *slides back one door and enters.*

BERT

Excuse me, Miss Helen. I didn't know no one was in here.

HELEN

(*Not looking up from cards*)

What did you want, Bert?

BERT

Just to see after the fire. Or did you aim to let this one go out? I laid one in the drawin' room for the company.

HELEN

And in the library?

BERT

Yes'm.

HELEN

Well, better keep this one going too. Lanny and some of us will want to sit back here after the guests arrive. And he mustn't get chilled or anything . . . Where is Lanny now, Bert?

BERT

He's out in the pantry having himself something more to eat. Nobody could guess now that boy was sick as he was this afternoon.

HELEN

(*Still looking at cards*)

He's all right now.

BERT

(*Sliding door closed*)

I hasn't never seen these doors shut before. Them painters didn't even paint 'em when they did the room.

HELEN

No, I didn't think then we'd ever ... want to close them.

BERT

It makes the place seem more old-timey and like back home, don't it, to be shutting doors between rooms downstairs. That, and having fires going in so many rooms. (*Goes to the fireplace and puts a log from the basket onto the fire*) I like fires myself, specially when you don't need 'em to keep warm but just has them for show.

HELEN

Stop chattering so, Bert.

BERT

Yes'm. I thought maybe my talking would keep things from seeming so gloomy in here. (*Moving to center*) You want me to clean up this mess on the ping-pong table?

HELEN

(*Impatiently*)

It doesn't matter. No. None of the guests will be back here. Bert, you are a regular magpie tonight.

BERT

(*Moving to door, center, extremely polite*)

Where is Mr. William going?

(HELEN *looks up and stares at him in silence for a moment.*)

BERT

He's been packing up his things for two, three days.

HELEN

(*Angry*)

So that's the backstairs gossip! So that's what's on your mind, Bert?

BERT

(*Contrite*)

Miss Helen, I didn't mean nothing. I thought maybe you—

HELEN

I know, Bert; I'm sorry for blowing up at you. That's what is on all our minds tonight ... You go along, Bert. Emmaline and the others will need your help. There are sixty or seventy people coming here tonight, and the banquet must have been over long ago.

(*One of the doors slides open very slowly. Enter* JAMES.)

133

BERT

They has already begun coming.

JAMES

Who shut these infernal doors? . . . And how about a little light?

(*He lights another lamp, just inside door, then comes forward a few steps.* HELEN *rises and walks toward him, slowly at first. Suddenly she hurries to him, puts her arms about his neck, hides her face in his shirt front. Exit* BERT, *closing the door after him.*)

JAMES

Helen, dear? Lanny's all right?

HELEN

Yes, but how long you've been gone. This evening has been an eternity.

JAMES

I shouldn't have left you here. I shouldn't have gone . . .

HELEN

One of us *had* to go. And one of us *had* to stay.

JAMES

We should have called off . . . having all these people here. If you don't feel like going in, there's Auntie Bet and Flo and Lucy. They—

HELEN

(*Suddenly*)

How is Lucy?

JAMES

(*Shrugs*)

. . . Is William . . . home?

HELEN

(*Shakes her head*)

I'll feel like going in presently. It is all right now that you are here, but oh, the thoughts I have thought tonight (*Cheering*) or almost thought—*would* have thought except for old Sol.

JAMES

Thoughts about William? . . . No, you mean about Lanny.

HELEN

About everybody in this house except thee and me, darling.

JAMES

And *some*times thou didst wonder about me?

HELEN

Never.

JAMES

What I've wondered tonight, Helen, is, was the world made for the likes of them or the likes of us?

HELEN

You've been alone too, haven't you, James?

(*Enter* AUNTIE BET *and* FLO DEAR, *center.* FLO DEAR *seems winded*.)

AUNTIE BET

These dreadful doors, Helen. Why in the world? And fires in every fireplace!

HELEN

I thought we'd have a little party within the party, back here.

AUNTIE BET

It was all Flo could do to get that door open.

FLO DEAR

I hope we are not intruding.

HELEN

Indeed you are not, Flo Dear. This is where the clan is going to gather. I see nothing against a friendly little game later on—perhaps poker.

JAMES

We do have a house full of guests, Helen.

HELEN

Oh, but the guests have Cousin Cameron. That's all they care about.

AUNTIE BET

How *is* everything, Helen?

HELEN

Everything was out in the pantry eating, at last report. He's all right, Auntie Bet. (*Patting her hand*) ... The banquet must have been a great success to have lasted so long.
(*Silence.*)

FLO DEAR

The food was delicious. I am sure they sent down home somewhere for that ham they served, and the spiced round.

HELEN

(*Looking at them in turn*)
And Cousin Cameron's speech?

AUNTIE BET

It was aw-w-wful.

HELEN

(*Laughing*)
Why, Auntie Bet, he's a spellbinder.

AUNTIE BET

Not tonight.

HELEN

You just weren't in the mood.
(JAMES *is lighting his pipe.*)

AUNTIE BET

Oh, it was awful.

137

HELEN

I'll bet Flo Dear didn't think so.

FLO DEAR

Well, it wasn't really so very bad once he got started, and if he hadn't lasted for so long—once he got started. He spoke for over an hour, dear. If you don't mind my saying so.

HELEN

Oh, *did* he? . . . James! Was it really so awful?

JAMES

It was awful long.

AUNTIE BET

I never saw any *field* hand consume so much food, or any *bounder* so much whiskey.

JAMES

Hold on, Auntie Bet. The Senator didn't really drink so much. He is just the old-timey toddy-drinking type. He'll get a little high off two or three shots, then sober up completely, then do it all over again. The truth is I don't believe he has ever been drunk in his life. With *his* constitution he can drink as much as he likes. He's made of iron. They don't make us like that any more.

FLO DEAR

Lucy drank quite a bit herself. I can't stand to see a woman drink.

AUNTIE BET

Never mind about Lucy, Flo.

HELEN

Poor Lucy.

JAMES

She drank a good deal, but she certainly didn't show it.

FLO DEAR

That's what I mean, James. *That* was the scandalous *thing!*

AUNTIE BET

There didn't used to be so much drinking at the Tennessee Society.

FLO DEAR

I'm not sure I'll go another year.

JAMES

(*Walking away in disgust*)

The ladies are exaggerating, Helen. It wasn't nearly so bad as they paint it.

AUNTIE BET

Perhaps not, James. But you cannot deny that when Senator Caswell stood up to speak he was quite unsteady.

FLO DEAR

I was a little frightened.

AUNTIE BET

And I can assure you he didn't speak a line of what he had prepared. He rambled on for an hour and a quarter about his childhood during the Civil War, and ended by talking about his mother—or his father, you could hardly tell which. Or *I* couldn't.

FLO DEAR

I am afraid no one could.

HELEN

What a shame. It is very well I didn't go . . . (*They are silent a moment*) Did Jim and Nancy get there all right?

JAMES

(*From across the room*)

They turned up, but they turned up very late—and she in your nineteen-twenties outfit. And then they made a very conspicuous departure in the middle of the Senator's speech.

AUNTIE BET

It was awful.

HELEN

They're head over heels in love, those two. Jim came to my room before they left for the tea dance, full of filial devotion and mumbling all kinds of confidences. (*Laughing*) Not at all himself.

(*Enter* LANNY, *from left, in dressing gown.*)

JAMES

Lanny!

(*The three women turn and face* LANNY. *He advances with a bouncing step.*)

LANNY

Most of the people have come. I've been watching and listening from the pantry.

JAMES

I hope no one saw you in that getup.

LANNY

No, I just kept the swinging door cracked a little. They are the weirdest assortment of people I have ever seen. And how they are gobbling up the food on the sideboard. You wouldn't think they had just come from a banquet.

JAMES

I imagine they would have found you a pretty weird sight.

HELEN

And you've been gobbling all evening.

LANNY

What I mean to say is, they're the weirdest *mixture* of people. Everyone's in evening clothes, but some of the women's dresses look like Halloween. Really!

HELEN

You don't include the dress Lucy is wearing, by any chance?

LANNY

Oh, Lucy and some of the others look like they were straight from Paris. That's the point. And there is just the same difference among the men. There is one priceless guy with an old-time tuxedo collar—this high. He can hardly turn his head around. But the funny thing is he kept talking on and on to a man in a very smooth dinner jacket, straight from De Pinna.

HELEN

(*Laughing*)

The man in the collar must be that Mr. Johnson. He has a grocery store out on Delmar. I noticed him last year.

JAMES

The De Pinna man is undoubtedly Hugh L. Martin. They're both from Dyersburg.

AUNTIE BET

(*Shaking her head*)

A very diverse group, Lanny—in your eyes—but Tennesseans all.

LANNY

How wonderful it was to see Cousin Cameron with them ... I could see straight through the dining room and into the library where people kept crowding around him. Sometimes I could almost catch what he was saying, though never quite. The rooms are full of people and yet now and then I could distinguish the sound of his voice among all the rest. What a splendid voice he has! Any stranger, just seeing him there and hearing him as I did, could tell he is something special. Every now and then when his voice rose above the others I would watch the faces of the people standing around the table in the dining room. When they heard him they would look at each other and you could tell how they felt about him ... If I were a painter I'd paint a picture of him and call it "The Last—" ... uh, "The Last—" ... something.

JAMES

In Tennessee they call him the last of the old-time orators.

FLO DEAR

Our county newspaper once called him "an American Lamartine." (*Dreamily*) And it went on to say, I remember: "He is not a man. He is a harp."

HELEN

I like that, Flo Dear.

AUNTIE BET

Perhaps it should be "The Last Southerner," Lanny.

LANNY

No, not that exactly. But what a feeling he gives one. Of seeing something you will never see duplicated, never repeated, that there isn't any more of. You know, he *is* what I thought old gentlemen in the South might be like. He is so honorable and disinterested.

HELEN

Lanny, really, you haven't seen enough of Cousin Cameron to form any such opinions. That's what you *wanted* him to be like.

LANNY

That's what he *is* like. But it still seems a little incredible that he really *came* here and that he *is* like that. It proves something for me . . . I like the way he keeps everything impersonal. If he isn't really a great man, he gives you an idea of what a great man must be like. He proves to me that there is such a thing.

JAMES

Lanny, you have a way of striking absurd and completely un-realistic attitudes toward people whom you hardly know, peo-ple who . . . are not at all available to you. You get just too entirely worked up. Now calm down.

LANNY

Why, it's something to get excited about, isn't it? Even when he wouldn't have anything to do with me last night and today, it didn't make me think any less of him. And just before he left for the banquet he stopped by my room and said we must have a talk when he got back. I *knew* something would happen to give me a chance to talk to him. "You can give a first impetus to events; afterwards they carry you along with them."

JAMES

Do you know what you are *saying?*

LANNY

I mean that it was I who put the Confederate flag above the mantelpiece in Cousin Cameron's room.

JAMES

If I thought for a minute that you put us through that hell this afternoon just for something like this!

HELEN

(*Going to* LANNY)

No, he didn't mean that, James. Listen, Lanny, we might as well get it over with. Sooner or later you must tell us what you had on your mind this afternoon, for our own peace of mind.

LANNY

(*Turning away*)

I don't want to talk about it. I don't know why I did it. It seems like something so *long* ago.

AUNTIE BET

We must go, Flo Dear. We promised Lucy to come right back in.

JAMES

No, Auntie Bet. Wait . . . We don't want to harass you, son . . . But *when* did you take those pills from Auntie Bet's room? She is entitled to hear whatever you will tell us. How did you happen to think of doing such a thing?

(*Silence.*)

LANNY

(*Fidgeting*)

It was just before lunch . . . I had opened the door to Uncle Brother's room—to see if something Bert had told me was true. Just when I was closing the door again I heard someone on the

stairway. I could tell it was Uncle Brother. The quickest place
I could get to was Auntie Bet's room, and I knew she and Flo
Dear had already gone downstairs. I waited in there till he went
back downstairs, and I was feeling depressed and . . . Where *is*
Uncle William? . . . Where *is* he? Lucy's in there with Cousin
Cameron and the company, but *he's* not in there.

HELEN

What Bert had told you about Brother turned out to be true,
didn't it, Lanny?

LANNY

Yes, it did. Where is he?

HELEN

He went downtown to his office for a while, after Lucy went
to the banquet.

LANNY

That's what you think, Mother. He has left town. He's gone.
Oh, what a joke on everybody.

AUNTIE BET

Lanny, William may not be going anywhere after all.

LANNY

If he's not gone already, he *is* going.

HELEN

(*Turning and walking to fireplace*)
Lanny, we are not going to listen to you talk about Uncle

Brother any more. You just get yourself worked up. Don't listen to him, James.

LANNY

He's going, and you all know it and you take it just as calmly as if it didn't matter. He's running off and leaving Lucy, and you act as though it were perfectly all right. Even Lucy does. After all the years she has put up with him. And he's leaving her without a penny—I'm sure of it—though she has worked as hard as he at the agency. What will become of her? She won't stay around here.

JAMES

Lanny, your uncle is a grown man, capable of—

LANNY

Capable of *anything*! Capable of *not* clearing out even. That would be the best joke of all.

JAMES

It's none of our business.

HELEN

What can your father or any of us do?

LANNY

Somebody ought to kill him.

HELEN

Yes, that's all this day needs, isn't it, Flo Dear?

FLO DEAR

Lanny, child—

(AUNTIE BET *rests a hand on* FLO DEAR'S *arm. They go out, center.* JAMES *goes and mixes himself a drink. Enter* JIM *and* NANCY, *right, carrying their wraps—* NANCY *in the twenties costume.*)

NANCY

Lanny, honey, how divine you're downstairs. You don't look a bit sick. Isn't it grand, Cousin Helen?

HELEN

Yes, it's grand, Nancy.

NANCY

(*To* LANNY)

Let me give you a big kiss. (*Kisses him*) How do you like my dress?

(*She whirls about.*)

LANNY

It's all right except it's so hideous.

NANCY

Oh, I don't care what I look like tonight. I feel so glorious. It is beginning to snow outside—a real Yankee snow. Snow always makes you feel so safe and snug and sure of yourself . . . You know, I am beginning to feel like I really belong here . . . Jimmy, why are you so silent? Aren't you going to tell them? I thought you wanted to shout it from the housetops.

(*Silence.* JIM *stands smiling at* NANCY.)

148

HELEN

How was the tea dance—the twenties party this afternoon?
Did everybody Charleston?

NANCY

It was the grandest party I have ever been to. (*Sentimenally*) I shall always remember it.

JAMES

Flapper parties were always a success.

NANCY

I'm glad I wore your dress on this special occasion, Cousin
Helen.

HELEN

I'm glad too. And Lucy wore my newest number to the banquet. She looks better in it than I do, and you certainly look better than I ever did in that number, Nancy.

JIM

(*Sotto voce, to* NANCY)
I told you they wouldn't listen.

HELEN

Stop muttering, Jim.

NANCY

(*To* LANNY, *who has wandered away from the group*)
Lanny, I attended the *banquet* in *this* dress. You should have
seen the looks I got.

LANNY

I don't know why. Compared to some of the dresses, yours must have looked quite up to date.

JIM

(*Sotto voce, to* NANCY)

They don't want to know. They would be happier if we would just elope.

NANCY

(*Aloud*)

You're so romantic, Jimmy.

> (WILLIAM *has entered, from right, with suitcase.* LANNY *stares at him. Enter* SENATOR CASWELL, *center. The eyes of all but* LANNY *and* WILLIAM *turn to* SENATOR CASWELL.)

HELEN

Ah, the guest of honor, to whom I owe all apologies.

SENATOR CASWELL

In yonder I am the guest of honor, Helen. I understand from Miss Betty there is another guest of honor back here. Oh, there's the fellow over there. Young fellow, I've just learned that this is the eve of your birthday.

NANCY

(*As* JIM *leads her out, center*)

It's the *evening* of his birthday, Granddaddy . . . (SENATOR CASWELL *looks at* NANCY *blankly*) . . . He wanted to hear it that way.

> (*She and* JIM *go out.* LANNY *continues to stare at* WILLIAM, *who has stopped near the rear wall, right.*)

JAMES

Lanny, your Cousin Cameron is speaking to you.

LANNY

(*Still staring at* WILLIAM)

It's a little late, isn't it?

(JAMES *moves toward* LANNY, *bristling*.)

HELEN

(*Covering up*)

I couldn't get to the banquet, Cousin Cameron, but I did mean to be in there to receive you and the others just now. I am the poorest kind of hostess.

SENATOR CASWELL

Dear lady, I have seen the quantities of food which you have laid out for us. It looks most delectable, most delectable. I can imagine it must have kept you occupied till this minute.

HELEN

You are very observant and very understanding.

SENATOR CASWELL

Well, you must excuse *me* for bursting in upon you all like this . . . (*His eyes on* LANNY) One must, especially, make allowances for the eccentricities of the aged . . . I am taking an early morning train tomorrow, and I wanted to say good night before any one of you went off to bed.

JAMES

(*Sotto voce, to* LANNY)

You go and make your apologies to Senator Caswell.

LANNY

(*Sotto voce, still staring at* WILLIAM)

I'd like to, Father, but what's the use? I didn't mean *he* was too late, but somehow he *is* too late now.

JAMES

You do as I say.

LANNY

(*Finally looking away from* WILLIAM *for the first time since* WILLIAM *entered*)

I am sorry if I seemed rude, Cousin Cameron. I thank you for coming back to tell me good night.

WILLIAM

(*In a loud voice that startles everyone*)

Lanny meant it was me who was a little late, Senator.

SENATOR CASWELL

Ah, William. I had not seen you there.
(*Enter* LUCY, *center.*)

LUCY

(*In doorway*)

Why, has William returned? Oh, so he has.

SENATOR CASWELL

Well, well, Miss Lucy!

LUCY

(LUCY *speaks more rapidly than she did in the first three acts, and her voice is pitched slightly higher*)

Don't look so surprised, Senator Caswell. I told you that I would look in on you back here in case of an explosive situation. It looks explosive to me . . . Don't you think some of us might go back to the company?

HELEN

WILLIAM

Lan, I didn't think anybody would be back here at this hour. I thought you would have hit the hay.

LANNY

And I thought you would be . . . on your way. Why aren't you?

WILLIAM

Well, for the time being I *am* going to make myself scarce. And it might not be a bad idea if—

HELEN

If we all did likewise, Brother?

SENATOR CASWELL

Wait, I beg of you.

LANNY

No, don't go!

Simultaneously

WILLIAM

They've both gotten cold feet!

LUCY

A little private chat won't hurt either of you.

153

SENATOR CASWELL

It wasn't to bust up this family party I came back here, and I—I won't have it so. I came merely to wish this boy a happy birthday.

WILLIAM

But that's not what "this boy" wishes, Senator. He wants to hear you talk about old times on the Cumberland Plateau or along the Tennessee River, about—

SENATOR CASWELL

About his family, you mean, and the country and the times they came out of. Yes, because he imagines deep inside him that he will discover a great generalization which—

WILLIAM

Come off it, Senator. Haven't you made one speech tonight? ... Give the Senator about two fingers, James.

HELEN

William, don't be insufferable.

LUCY

Oh, Helen, he's right. Lanny is entitled to something a little more solid . . . It's the recollections of your lifetime he wants, Senator Caswell.

SENATOR CASWELL

Yes, James, about two fingers . . . I am afraid that some of us here do the boy an injustice. It is not merely family and history that worry him. It is something broader. It is a philosophical point the boy is after ... Thank you, James.

WILLIAM

(*To* LUCY)

This is worse than I thought possible.

SENATOR CASWELL

(*Turning up glass*)

It is something like this: the conflict between love of particular things and love of the general. For any man the greatest generalization of all is himself. And the particularity he loves is not in himself but in the things and people he seems to possess . . . and by which, despite all he may do, he *is* possessed.

(*Silence.*)

WILLIAM

(*Applauding*)

More! More!

LUCY

No, that's enough. To those people at the banquet the Senator poured forth his memories, and he saved his speech-making for Lanny. He is a deep one, William. I suppose he intended to confuse us all, and he has.

HELEN

You are among Philistines, Cousin Cameron. But I appreciate what you said. And I am sure that Lanny does . . . (*As she goes to* JAMES *and takes his arm*) And now we certainly must make an appearance in there.

LUCY

Yes, Senator, your admirers in there will be getting restless. They will be whispering that James and Helen have secreted

you somewhere. One lady had already asked me before I left if
James and Helen thought they had some particular claim on
you just because you happened to be staying in their house this
year. It seems you were her guest year before last. I wonder—
have you claimed next year's kin?

HELEN

Lucy, that's not like you.

SENATOR CASWELL

(*Quietly smiling*)

The public is a jealous mistress . . . (*To* LANNY *and* WIL-
LIAM, *who are not looking at him*) Good-bye, my friends. I
am taking an early train tomorrow. Forgive my philosophizing.
I am an old man . . . an old covite . . . an old nonagenarian almost. Under different circumstances—

HELEN

Come along, Cousin Cameron.
(*Exeunt* HELEN *and* JAMES.)

WILLIAM

(*Moving to center*)

Good-bye, Senator. No hard feelings?
(*They shake hands. Suddenly* SENATOR CASWELL *turns
toward* LANNY, *crosses the room to him. A silence. They
stand looking at each other.* SENATOR CASWELL *sits down in
a straight chair facing* LANNY, *who remains standing as
before.*)

SENATOR CASWELL

There was a man when I was a boy, the oldest man I ever
knew and the blackest.

WILLIAM

(*Sotto voce*)

Well, we've won the day, Lucy, after all.

LUCY

(*Sotto voce*)

Yes, for what it's worth, William.

(WILLIAM *turns his back to* LUCY, *watching* SENATOR
CASWELL. *Slowly* LUCY *covers her face with her hands,
only lowering them after the* SENATOR *has spoken several sentences.*)

SENATOR CASWELL

The man's name was Prince. They called him Prince because
he claimed to be the son of a Congo chieftain and, before he
was taken into slavery, himself the heir apparent of the tribe.
So he said, and I do not doubt that this was so. He had the
noblest bearing of any man I have ever known. By his own
reckoning he was a hundred and fourteen years old the year he
died. People said he had been at New Orleans in 1812 with my
grandfather. They even said that he had ridden out with my
great-grandfather to hear Sam Doakes preach the Sword of
the Lord and of Gideon before King's Mountain. That may
be so, too. But the stories he regaled us boys on the farm
with were stories of his youth in the jungles—of lion hunts and
tribal warfare. Why, I used to lie awake nights wishing that *I*

could have been born to such a life. It seemed to me then that it would have been worth a hundred years of slavery to have known one day of that noble, carefree existence which Prince described. The greatest loyalty I have ever felt in my breast was what I felt for the Ubwangi, the ever watchful Ubwangi tribe; and I have never since known such loathing as I felt for the despised Wulu people. Even after old Prince was dead and I was almost a man, I was haunted by his stories and was sometimes filled with a senseless longing to go to some faraway place and live the life of the noble savage. It is possible, of course, that old Prince made up those tales out of the whole cloth, for his own satisfaction, and meaning no harm by it. Who could ever prove the truth or untruth of what he said—things that had happened a hundred years back on the other side of the world. Anyway, they were fine stories for boys to hear . . . But, you know, even as a little fellow I knew somehow that when I held converse with Prince it was not with a man who had been a boy a hundred years back but, as far as I was concerned, a thousand years back, perhaps ten thousand years. That was something self-evident; there was no confusion in our minds about it . . . (*Standing*) But, you see, that would not have been so with you and me. I would have talked to you about old times back home as though it was all day before yesterday, as you no doubt believe it was. But it isn't so! By any sensible reckoning of history there are a thousand years between your generation and mine. (*Begins to leave*) Son, a man who was born in 1854 is older than any of the persons assembled in this house tonight has yet dared to dream. And in another decade or two, even such a meeting as that one I addressed tonight—if anyone recalls it— will seem like something out of an age ancient and remote.

(*He makes a vague, despairing gesture, almost a salute,
to* LANNY *and repeats it several times as he goes out.*
LANNY *remains standing, as before.*)

LUCY

Lanny, you ought to have said *something*. After all, your
Cousin Cameron made a valiant effort.

LANNY

Cousin Cameron!
 (*He laughs and takes up a cigarette from the box on
 the table.*)

LUCY

Oh, put down that cigarette, Lanny. Give it to me. Your
mother and father will be back any moment.

WILLIAM

What you need now, Lan, is a good night's sleep.

LANNY

"To sleep, perchance to dream!" . . . (*Gesturing*) "Macbeth
doth murder sleep!"

LUCY

Cut it out, Lanny! You don't frighten us. You're over the
hump. We all are. Listen to me now. From here out we three
are going to speak a different language. We are going to look
at things differently. Before they send you off to bed, James and
Helen want to have a little private family celebration. They
think it might cheer you and make you sleep better to exchange

birthday and anniversary presents tonight . . . I want you to be sensible. I want you to begin using your head.

LANNY

As though I haven't always.

WILLIAM

Lucy means something different, Lanny. She and I want you . . . to make tonight as easy as possible for everybody. We think maybe things are going to be different soon. Lucy and I are going to get married, Lan. Right away.

LANNY

You're what?

WILLIAM

And get us a house, probably right in this block.
(LUCY *nods assent, her eyes on* LANNY.)

LANNY

(*Laughing*)
Lucy wouldn't live in the same house with you! (*Now serious*) You were going to pull out on her. Your bags are packed. Do you think everybody doesn't know what's in that suitcase? Why, I'll—
(*Suddenly he seizes the glass cigarette box and starts toward* WILLIAM. LUCY *stops him.*)

LUCY

Don't you know you couldn't hurt him? (LANNY *moves to fireplace, left*) . . . What I was trying to tell you, Lanny, is that

160

with your parents you can be only a son. And so it behooves
you to make the most of that—not just dutifully, but with self-
interest. You have to play it their way, Lanny.

WILLIAM

What are you saying to him, Lucy?

LUCY

I am trying to tell him that he didn't ask to be born in an up-
rooted country family here in this meaningless place. I want
him to see that it owes him whatever he can salvage out of the
situation. Just what it owes us—which is everything.

WILLIAM

Hell, you don't think that, Lucy.

LUCY

That's why I am going to marry you, isn't it, William? Incidentally, I am in love with you, but incidentally Lanny loves his
parents and they love him. Yet in the final analysis—for *me*
and for *you*—that is neither here nor there . . . The debt you
owe me, William, is so enormous that no mere house on Lindell
Boulevard will begin to pay it. Membership in a thousand
country clubs would not begin. And the more you try to pay on
this debt to me, William, the more you will owe me.

WILLIAM

God! Surely I'm asleep again. This is worse than any dream
I've ever had, Lucy.

LUCY

Let's be realistic about how matters stand, William.

WILLIAM

Why are you saying all this? You don't believe a word of it.

LUCY

Oh, I do believe it. I believe with all my soul that I have an everlasting claim on you. Whatever else I may believe or feel, I feel what I have just said so deeply that nothing could ever change it. However much I may despise myself for it, I know that I shall feel every year that you owe me more and more. Every payment would only increase the debt.

(LANNY *stares at* LUCY.)

WILLIAM

I said today you had changed. But I didn't know the half of it.

LUCY

But you opened my eyes to the whole of it, William, by offering me what was only mine by rights.

WILLIAM

By *rights?*

LUCY

You had better believe your ears this time, William.

WILLIAM

(*As he is going out with suitcase, right*)
What I owe you, Lucy, is already in the First National Bank. Today I withdrew everything from my account at James' place

of business. Half of it is now deposited in your name at the
First National. The other half is right here. Tell Jim he'll find
my car at the airport if he wants it—but not me or the money.
(*Looking at the clock*) My God, there *is* time.

(*Exit* WILLIAM.)

LANNY

Uncle Brother, you fool!

LUCY

Hurry, William. Hurry, before I follow you.

LANNY

Lucy!

LUCY

Call me Aunt Lucy. I am a rich old maid now, with a will
that may be changed any day of the week. And now I must
join Auntie Bet and Flo Dear . . . in there at the party, I mean
. . . I promised them I would come back.

LANNY

Only Uncle Brother could have been taken in by what you
just did, Lucy. You *made* him go on without you.

LUCY

I made him go on by confessing the truth to him.

LANNY

Oh, there wasn't a word of truth in what you said.

LUCY

I wish we could leave it at that. At six o'clock this evening—

LANNY

You sent him off so he wouldn't be trapped here. You were very obvious. You wanted him to stay. You were pretty obvious about that too.

LUCY

At six o'clock this evening everything you are saying would have been, or seemed, true.

LANNY

You felt that if he didn't get away tonight he might never get away.

LUCY

Don't . . . don't let's be tiresome, Lanny. That is only how it seems to *you*.

LANNY

Am I being tiresome?

LUCY

One of us is. I must go back to the party.

LANNY

Won't the party seem tiresome too? Won't everything seem tiresome to you? William's gone. And you couldn't catch him now if you tried. And he won't ever come back. Or ever send for you, Lucy. He has cleared out.

LUCY

You can't understand why I don't break down and weep now that he is gone. Truly that was the way it should have been and would have been a few hours ago. But something happened.

LANNY

He did one last damned thing? That even you couldn't take?

LUCY

No . . . Yes, yes, he did. He changed his mind. He was going to stay. We were going to reach a new understanding. For a while I thought maybe we could, and then I saw we couldn't. And then I began making up those things that I would say to him to make him go. As you say, it was pretty obvious. It was pretty easy . . . with William.

LANNY

I knew you made them up.

LUCY

Yes, I rehearsed them all evening, over and over. I said them over and over to myself, and then finally the thing happened.

LANNY

Yes.

LUCY

I began to understand that the things I was going to say were truly what I felt.

LANNY

No, there is no truth in that either.

LUCY

It was what I felt only in some small degree, deep, deep down, only in a special sense and in a small degree—but enough. Any was too much. The simple fact is it was too late for William and me to marry. The time had passed. I did what I did, for myself.

LANNY

But it wasn't the country club or the house on Lindell Boulevard you felt he owed you ... It was something else, wasn't it?

LUCY

(*Quietly*)

It was you.

LANNY

Yes, I know.

LUCY

It was you that William and I were going to get hold of. William and I are nothing to each other any more, Lanny. But if we could have got hold of you, we would have had a common interest—that is, we could have begun deceiving ourselves, at your expense. Didn't you see us arranging matters for you with the Senator, the way we thought they ought to be. We would have been no different from your two aunts. We would have been more dangerous.

LANNY

Then it's *me* you've saved.

LUCY

Nobody's ever saved, Lanny—not from this kind of danger, not except for the moment. And even then nobody ever saves anybody but himself. It was I who was in the worst danger to-day. It is I who am saved for the moment.

LANNY

Lucy, can't you come here and live with us now? I can promise you that I would never make it difficult for you by saying silly things like those I said this morning.

LUCY

I know you wouldn't, Lanny. That's all changed for you, isn't it? (*He doesn't answer*) . . . No, I'm going to do the usual thing for a woman in my position. I have money, and I am going to travel. William thinks he has gone to where there is a new kind of wealth and perhaps a new kind of life. Well, even if he is right, it won't last. Your family has been here only one generation, and it's all over with already. At least I shall head out in the opposite direction from William. That's inevitable. (*Trying to brighten*) Anyhow, I shall go by way of the party, Lanny. I am sure your mother and the others are only waiting for me to come and release them—so they can come back here to you. Good night, Lanny, and happy birthday. I'm afraid I haven't a present for you, after all.

LANNY

Nothing, Lucy? I thought—

167

LUCY

Nothing. Nothing from me to you. You'll have enough to remember this day by.

LANNY

Don't go yet, Lucy. Cousin Cameron and Uncle Brother—and now you're clearing out. When you go—

LUCY

When I go you'll be on your own.

LANNY

When you go I'll be alone here.

LUCY

All the others will be in here in a moment full of merriment and loaded with presents for you.

LANNY

(*Turning away*)

God, yes! And I am going to be the merriest of them all.

LUCY

Yes, I know you will. *You* cleared out sometime this evening, Lanny, before any of the rest of us. We are only following in your wake.

> (*Exit* LUCY. LANNY *turns and sees that she has gone. He stands staring toward the doorway until* HELEN *appears there followed by* JAMES, *and presently by* NANCY *and* JIM.)

HELEN

Happy birthday, Lan!

JAMES

(*Moving toward closet, right*)

Yes, many happy returns!

HELEN

(*Kissing* LANNY's *cheek*)

A quarter says you can't guess what I've got for you. (LANNY *continues to stand perfectly still, facing the doorway.* HELEN *snaps her fingers before his eyes*) Lanny! . . . Happy birthday. Many happy returns.

LANNY

(*As though just becoming aware of their presence*)

Oh, the same to both of you, but my presents are upstairs.

HELEN

So are mine. I've sent Bert to fetch them, and he can go back for yours. (*Enter* BERT *with arms full of packages, from left*) Ah, here he is. Thank you, Bert. Now will you get Lanny's for him?

LANNY

They are all under my bed, Bert, except one little one behind the books on my top shelf.

HELEN

A *little* one? Not for me I hope.

LANNY

No, it's my unbirthday present for Auntie Bet.

BERT

(*Going out left*)

I know exactly where they are.

LANNY

How do you know?

HELEN

He knows because he's not supposed to know.

BERT

(*Snickering as he goes out*)

Aw, Miss Helen.

(JAMES *has brought out golf clubs in their wrappings, and hoisted them onto ping-pong table. As he does so—*)

HELEN

James, for *me?*

JAMES

No. Sorry, dear. For Lanny. But I have yours right here in the closet. (*He turns toward the closet again, but stops*) By George! As usual I forgot that we include Auntie Bet and Flo Dear.

HELEN

And as usual I got something for you to give them.

LANNY

They're coming back here too?

JAMES

Of course they are, Lanny.

LANNY

Oh, of course they are.

HELEN

Isn't all this for them more than for anybody else, Lanny?

JAMES

What *is* it I'm giving them, Helen?

HELEN

I can't even remember what I'm giving them. It's a case of shopping *too* early. I bought and wrapped all these things before I packed away my Christmas ribbons.

(JAMES *brings out a second package from the closet.*)

JAMES

Well, anyway, there won't be time for the usual guessing game.

HELEN

Who says there won't? What's the use of exchanging presents if you don't have a chance to guess what you're getting?

JAMES

We do have a house full of company waiting.

HELEN

Oh, forget the company!

LANNY

Yes, let 'em eat cake!

HELEN

That's the spirit, Lanny. We are going to make a real competition of it, like at Christmas. Everybody will get one good look and one good feel of each of his presents. Then we'll pile them all on the table and open them one by one, and keep score. Try this, Lanny.

LANNY

(*Accepting package*)

Do we get a shake?

HELEN

The choice between a shake and a squeeze.

LANNY

I'll take a shake ... It's a chess set? ... Chinese checkers? ... Dominoes? ... Mah-jong?

(*While the conversation continues, enter* NANCY *center, followed immediately by* JIM, *carrying presents.* LANNY *is at the table placing the present from* HELEN *beside that from* JAMES, *facing the audience.*)

JAMES

This is for you, Helen.

HELEN

Mmmmmm. It's heavy.

JAMES
(*Reading tags*)

Let's see, this from me to Flo—

LANNY
(*Feeling his present from* JAMES)

Umbrellas?

NANCY

Happy birthday, Lanny.

LANNY

That glorious girl is here!

JIM

None of your sarcasm.

LANNY

I mean it.

JAMES

Even Jim's been shopping.

JIM

Nancy *took* me.

HELEN

Jim, we are going to have the grand competition! Like at Christmas!

NANCY

Lanny, Jim and I have the biggest surprise for you of all. You'd never guess what.

173

HELEN

A quarter says he can.

JAMES

Be sure all bets are placed before—

(*Enter* FLO DEAR *and* AUNTIE BET, *left.* AUNTIE BET *has her arms full of presents.* FLO DEAR *pushes a teacart on which there is a large cake with candles lit. They call out: "Happy birthday!"*)

LANNY

Trial by fire.

(*All others join in singing "Happy Birthday." Enter* BERT, *center, with* LANNY'S *presents.* LANNY *goes and relieves him and distributes his presents.*)

JAMES

Blow out your candles, Lanny. Make a wish and blow them all out.

LANNY

What if I *can't.*

NANCY

You will, Lanny. Make your wish one for Jim and me.

LANNY

Tell me your surprise so I'll know what kind of wish to make.

NANCY

(*Taking* JIM'S *arm*)

Jim is going home with Granddaddy and me tomorrow to *meet* the family!

AUNTIE BET

Oh, I strongly suspected—
(*She hiccups.*)

BERT

(*Going to* HELEN)

Here, Miss Helen.

HELEN

What is it, Bert?
(BERT *hands her an envelope.*)

BERT

I don't know'm. Miss Lucy left it as she went out.

JAMES

As she went *out?*

BERT

Went out . . . (*Then to* HELEN) I was starting up to get
Lanny's presents, and she came scurrying down the back stairs
on tippytoes. She handed me this . . . and this (*Hands another
envelope to* JIM) I said was they presents, and she said yes she
guessed they was presents all right. And I said wasn't they one
for you, Lan, but she said no there wasn't and was gone—out
the back door. I reckon—

HELEN

(*Reading note*)

Never mind what you reckon, Bert . . . Oh, it's nothing. It's about my dress. She tore it a little getting out of it. (*Still reading*) ... What a shame.

> (*She passes the note to* JAMES.)

FLO DEAR

Yes, what a shame.

AUNTIE BET

> (*Hiccups*)

How careless of her.

NANCY

How thoughtless of her to tell you about it tonight. We were all so happy.

HELEN

Oh, it doesn't matter about the dress.

JAMES

> (*Holding note*)

Lucy has gone away.

JIM

Read this, Nancy! Uncle Brother has left us his convertible. It's at the airport with the key in it!

NANCY

> (*Taking* JIM's *note*)

Oh, Jimmy, Jimmy, we'll drive back to Tennessee in it! I can see us pulling up at home. I'm so happy. Why, I'm going to cry.

> (*She sinks down into a chair.*)

FLO DEAR

(*To* BERT, *who lingers in doorway*)
Bert, get Miss Betty a glass of soda. It's her indigestion.
(AUNTIE BET *is seated in a straight chair, hiccupping.*
JAMES *goes to her.* HELEN *goes to* NANCY. LANNY *peers between* HELEN *and* JIM *at* NANCY.)

LANNY

She's crying from pure joy.

HELEN

Lanny, go blow out your candles.

LANNY

I can't think what to wish.

JIM

(*Kneeling beside* NANCY)
Nancy, don't cry. I love you, Nancy dear. How wonderful it is.

JAMES

Lanny, didn't you hear your mother? Blow out your candles!
Do you want to set the house on fire?

LANNY

(*Stooping beside the cake, but only gazing at the candles, he
speaks slowly*)
Give me time. Give me time.
(*The candles burn on.*)

Curtain

ABOUT THE AUTHOR

PETER TAYLOR was born at Trenton, Tennessee, in 1917. He attended schools in Nashville, Memphis and St. Louis. In 1936 he entered Vanderbilt University at Nashville, and later he went to Kenyon College, where he was graduated in 1940. During the Second World War he served four years in the Army as an enlisted man. Two years after his discharge from the Army his first book, *A Long Fourth and Other Stories,* was published. This was a collection of stories that had appeared in *The Southern Review, The Partisan Review, The Kenyon Review* and *The Sewanee Review.* A second collection of his stories, *The Widows of Thornton,* was published in 1954. All but one of the stories in it had been printed in *The New Yorker.* A short novel entitled *A Woman of Means* was published in book form in 1950.

In 1952 Peter Taylor returned to Kenyon College, where he now teaches courses in the English and Drama departments. He has also held teaching appointments at Indiana University, The Woman's College of the University of North Carolina and The University of Chicago. In the summer of 1955 he was Lecturer in Creative Writing at the Conference in American Studies at University College, Oxford. His wife is Eleanor Ross Taylor. They have two children.